Humble Inquiry

Humble Inquiry

The Gentle Art of Asking Instead of Telling

SECOND EDITION | REVISED AND EXPANDED

EDGAR H. SCHEIN
and
PETER A. SCHEIN

Berrett–Koehler Publishers, Inc.

Berrett-Koehler Publishers, Inc.
1333 Broadway, Suite 1000
Oakland, CA 94612-1921
Tel: (510) 817-2277
Fax: (510) 817-2278
www.bkconnection.com

ORDERING INFORMATION

Quantity sales. Special discounts are available on quantity purchases by corporations, associations, and others. For details, contact the "Special Sales Department" at the Berrett-Koehler address above.

Individual sales. Berrett-Koehler publications are available through most bookstores. They can also be ordered directly from Berrett-Koehler: Tel: (800) 929-2929; Fax: (802) 864-7626; www.bkconnection.com.

Orders for college textbook/course adoption use. Please contact Berrett-Koehler: Tel: (800) 929-2929; Fax: (802) 864-7626.

Distributed to the U.S. trade and internationally by Penguin Random House Publisher Services.

Berrett-Koehler and the BK logo are registered trademarks of Berrett-Koehler Publishers, Inc.

Printed in the United States of America

Berrett-Koehler books are printed on long-lasting acid-free paper. When it is available, we choose paper that has been manufactured by environmentally responsible processes. These may include using trees grown in sustainable forests, incorporating recycled paper, minimizing chlorine in bleaching, or recycling the energy produced at the paper mill.

Library of Congress Cataloging-in-Publication Data

Names: Schein, Edgar H., author. | Schein, Peter A., author.
Title: Humble inquiry : the gentle art of asking instead of telling / Edgar H. Schein and Peter A. Schein.
Description: Second edition, revised and expanded. | Oakland, CA : Berrett-Koehler Publishers, [2021] | Includes bibliographical references and index.
Identifiers: LCCN 2020044400 | ISBN 9781523092628 (paperback ; alk. paper) | ISBN 9781523092635 (adobe pdf) | ISBN 9781523092642 (epub)
Subjects: LCSH: Interpersonal communication. | Interpersonal relations. | Organizational behavior. | Humility.
Classification: LCC BF637.C45 S352 2021 | DDC 155.4/136--dc23
LC record available at https://lccn.loc.gov/2020044400

Second Edition

30 29 28 27 26 25 24 23 22 21 | 10 9 8 7 6 5 4 3

Book producer: BookMatters; Copyeditor: Tanya Grove;
Cover designer: Susan Malikowski, DesignLeaf Studio

To Earth's doctors, nurses, care providers, and health care administrators who have worked so tirelessly to protect humanity during this horrible COVID-19 pandemic.

Contents

Preface to the Second Edition

The motivation to write a second edition of this book continues to be personal and professional for both of us. We can see in today's and tomorrow's world more reasons than ever why *Humble Inquiry*—the gentle art of asking questions to which we don't already know the answer—must be practiced to build better relationships and to help others to untangle the complex situations we are confronted with daily.

What is new in this second edition is a deepening and broadening of this concept, seeing it as both a set of guidelines for to how to ask better questions and as an entire attitude that includes better listening, better responding to what others are trying to tell us, and better revealing of ourselves to facilitate positive relationship building that leads to more effective problem-solving in our daily interactions. And we need to do more of this than ever because our cultural scripts continue to push us in the wrong direction, toward thinking we know the answer and feeling that it is appropriate to tell it to others as if it is *the truth*.

Is it inevitabile that as the world becomes more interlinked and multicultural, most of the time we do not know what is *really going on* or *why this is happening now?* We hope that the deeper and broader approach to Humble Inquiry presented here will help you to see around and through the brazen *telling* provided by others, and to deepen the skills to *learn* what really matters.

Keeping up with the content of accelerating change is really hard. Naturally we all share the inclination to focus on what we know, on our industry, or on our area of expertise, where we can be comfortable keeping up with what is changing. Yet trying to keep up with the *content* of accelerating change may actually be less important than keeping up with the *context* of accelerating change. There is a real difference between the content question "What changed?" and the context question "What is going on?" or "Why is this happening?"

This is particularly important now because, as strange as this sounds, our reactions to right and wrong, fact or opinion, truth or lies, have evolved since the first edition of this book came out in 2013. This second edition begins with the same incident of someone telling Ed something that was neither helpful nor true. The person doing the telling had a strong need to tell, with, no doubt, good intentions to be helpful. At that time, Ed's mild annoyance was the spark that lit the flame for the first edition, and the teller was easily forgiven for passionately expressing a point of view, even though the facts it was based on were not entirely accurate! The difference now, as we work on the second edition, is that the sense of what is truth and objective reality is *itself* being called into question with alarming regularity.

We have entered into a different relationship with right and wrong, with facts versus alternative facts, with empirical evidence versus opinion or belief. As long as humans have made decisions, we have formulated and relied upon these believed distinctions between right and wrong, reality and illusion. What has changed is that we are now more explicitly, or tribally, encouraged to challenge the other view, regardless of the empirical scientific evidence supporting either view. Have we come to believe, now more than ever, that *telling* is the way to lead?

Part of the acceleration of change, therefore, is the in-creased tendency to trust our passion about a belief, even sometimes in contradiction to the scientific basis. In the hyper-partisan and tribal public square, the *force* with which beliefs are expressed seems to matter even more than the *facts* and their basis in science. Whether it's climate cri-sis or pandemic—two profound challenges of our current physical world—the partisan perspective, or context, too often overpowers or outshouts the science in matters that have actual impact on our lives. It is as if inconvenient or threatening realities matter less than how rigidly, consis-tently, and tribally the alternative views are argued and dem-onstrated. For some, the point is more about winning the ar-gument, about "us" and "our view" than it is about truths that can be checked, verified, and agreed upon. It seems increas-ingly the case that the last thing that some want is to *agree* because there is more to be gained by continuing to amplify the argument and reinforce the division between "us" and "them." More than ever, the increased use of Humble Inquiry can become an essential learning process to collectively dis-cover the essential elements of shared experience that we can live with and progress within.

This global divisiveness has accelerated at least as fast as the rate of change we have experienced since the first edi-tion. What may be most perilous about this tribalism is that it makes it okay to not learn or relearn. If there is one ratio-nale we can offer above all for reading this book, it is this: through Humble Inquiry you can learn more about what is happening in your work and in your life, and you can learn to consistently *separate the signal from the noise*. In a world that inevitably confuses fact with alternative fact and fiction, we hope this book will help you learn in your conversations and relationships what really matters to the people you care about and need to care about. With added inquiry and reflection, you can also learn new things about yourself.

And Humble Inquiry might also help you relearn *how to learn*. You may discover that there is more actionable information in the details of what's *really going on* than in simply knowing what happened or what has changed. Relearning how to inquire, listen, reflect, and then act, is what the Humble Inquiry *attitude* is all about. A deep thinker about the future, Bob Johansen describes a polarity between *certainty* and *clarity*. Certainty is the belief and adherence to a point of view, often accompanied by vehement argument. Clarity is being able to see and learn more of what is really going on, the full spectrum of dimensions that emerge as critically important as events unfold.[1] We add that seeing with more clarity and abandoning certainty are benefits of a Humble Inquiry attitude.

To facilitate this learning, this edition provides new stories and illustrations to further illuminate the Humble Inquiry concept. You will also find more exercises and suggestions for learning and practicing Humble Inquiry. One thing that is not new but cannot be stressed enough is that Humble Inquiry is both an attitude and a process. It is not an algorithm or set of rules. Though the term itself is not new, the nuances and complications associated with practicing this form of communicating and relationship building can be applied in new situations everyday. We can all learn to be better humble inquirers.

Who Is This Book For?

This book is for anyone who is seeking more productive positive relationships, looking for new ways of understanding what is really going on, or wanting to be more helpful. Of course all of us could benefit from more productive relationships, new ways of understanding, and learning how to be more helpful. However, people in leadership roles particularly need to hone these skills because this art of inquiry becomes more challenging as power and status increase. Our culture emphasizes that leaders set direction and articulate values, all of which predisposes them to *tell* rather than *ask*. Yet it is such leaders who may need Humble Inquiry most because intricate interdependent tasks require building positive, open, and trusting relationships above, below, and around them, in order to facilitate safer and more effective task performance and innovation in the face of a perpetually changing context.

How This Book Is Organized

In the first few chapters we explain in greater detail what Humble Inquiry really means on a practical day-to-day basis. In Chapter 3 we sharpen this by contrasting Humble Inquiry with other forms of inquiry used by helpers and coaches. We dive into these questions: What are the social, cultural, and psychological forces at work that inhibit us from easy acceptance of this form of relationship building? To be humbly inquiring, what do we have to *unlearn* and *relearn* to be successful?

Chapter 4 digs into the cultural forces operating in us all the time, especially in the United States, and tries to show how this subtly encourages telling and inhibits Humble Inquiry. Chapter 5 elaborates this argument by analyzing how patterns in organizational hierarchies, and in society generally, create many of the "rules" that further complicate Humble Inquiry. These forces interact subtly with our own intrapsychic forces and cognitive biases to make open and honest conversations more challenging.

Chapter 6 examines in greater detail the subtle social dynamics of conversations, and Chapter 7 explores what happens inside our head in the few moments between when we observe something and when we react to it. All of this is intended to help you understand both why you may not be using Humble Inquiry when you should be, and what you might have to unlearn and relearn to improve your situational skills in conversations.

Chapter 8 provides a summary of where we have been and where we need to go. Last, we conclude the book with discussion suggestions and exercises that will help the reader learn how to differentiate asking from telling and build inquiry skills that will open communication and deepen relationships. Unlearning and relearning happen in small steps based on self-observation, reflection, trial and error, analysis, resetting goals, and continuing to learn. We hope this book will intrigue you and guide you on that path. How each of us adopts Humble Inquiry may be unique—it's not formulaic. And the process starts here.

Peter A. Schein and Edgar H. Schein
September 2020

Humble Inquiry

Introduction:
What Is Humble Inquiry?

It all started with a story that Ed has told many times in the last few years:

> I have never liked being told things gratuitously, especially things I already know. The other day I was admiring an unusual bunch of mushrooms that had grown after a heavy rain when an elderly woman walking her dog chose to stop.
>
> In a loud voice she said, "Some of those are poisonous, you know."
>
> I replied, "I know."
>
> She added, "Some of them can kill you, you know."
>
> I must have been a sight squatting down looking at this profusion of spring mushrooms, but to this day I still wonder why she didn't just wander over and ask, "What are you doing? What are you looking at?"
>
> What struck me was how her need to lecture me not only offended me but also made it difficult for me to respond in a positive manner. I realized that her tone and her "telling" approach prevented me from building a positive relationship and made further

communication awkward. Her motivation might have been to help me, yet I found it unhelpful and wished that she had asked me a question either at the beginning or after I said "I know," instead of trying to tell me something more, which was not even correct. These mushrooms would have given me indigestion, but they were not the deadly kind.

We find in this story one of the major problems of our time. We value telling each other things, showing off how much we know, and winning arguments, whether we're using verified data or not. Winning, being right, convincing others—these victories are so important to many people that they feel free to spin, invent, or lie because what is true and what is not true has become a matter of debate. Opinionated distortions—what may be considered tactical necessities in politics, where winning is indeed the most important thing—have crept into too much of our discourse about empirically measured reality.

Why are asking questions, and building positive relationships, suddenly so important?

Because in an increasingly volatile and culturally diverse world, we cannot hope to understand and work with people from different occupational, professional, and national cultures if we do not know how to ask questions and build relationships that are based on (1) the assumption that other values may be different but are no worse and no better than our own, and (2) we may need to know what others know in order to solve our own problems.

How We Define Humble Inquiry

An Art

Humble Inquiry is the fine art of drawing someone out, of asking questions to which you do not already know the answer, of building a relationship based on curiosity and interest in another person.

An Attitude

Humble Inquiry is not just asking questions; it is a total attitude that includes listening more deeply to how others respond to our inquiry, responding appropriately, and revealing more of ourselves in the relationship building process.

Humble Inquiry is a great way to connect to another person, to build a relationship.

There are many contexts in which productive relationships, completing work tasks—even helping others to save lives—absolutely depend on inquiring in the right way to figure out what is really going on. If you allow yourself to be really interested in what you don't know about another person, to be open to your natural curiosity, what more could you learn? Would this make it easier and more comfortable to reveal things about yourself that you are pretty sure the other person might be interested in? Would this be a new way of building relationships at work? *Inquiring* and *revealing in this way* are the key processes of displaying the Humble Inquiry attitude.

Humble Inquiry can help you make sense of complex situations that you do not or cannot understand on your own.

When a team is trying to solve a tricky problem of what to do next and is stuck among several alternatives, Humble Inquiry means asking, "*What else* do we need to know?" or "How did we/you arrive at this point?" This is particularly true when others propose something that we oppose or don't understand. It is asking the question, "How do we connect the dots to make sense of this predicament that we don't fully understand yet?"

Humble Inquiry helps involve others in problem-solving and decision-making by *helping them* to see a problem, to be clear about their motives in a given situation, or to articulate what kind of help they need from a friend or coach.

When you are asked for advice, do you jump in with a response, pitching your solution? An alternative Humble Inquiry approach might start with asking why advice is needed, why it is needed now, why it is you who is being asked for advice. The context may be much more important than the content of your response.

> The attitude of Humble Inquiry is based on curiosity, openness to the truth, and the recognition that insights most often come from conversations and relationships in which we have learned to listen to each other, and have learned to respond appropriately to make joint sense out of our shared context, rather than arguing each other into submission.

Does Humble Inquiry Require Embracing Humility in the Here-and-now?

Why is the word *humble* so important in this form of questioning? The Humble Inquiry attitude does not require that humility be a major *personality* trait of a good inquirer. But even the most confident or arrogant among us will find ourselves humbled by the reality of being dependent on others, and by the sheer complexity of trying to figure out what is important and what is not. We can think of this as *Here-and-now Humility*, accepting our dependence on each for information sharing and task completion.

Displaying Here-and-now Humility is one key to building positive relationships with those upon whom we are dependent because it reveals our genuine interest and curiosity in others as critical partners. The ability to embrace Here-and-now Humility, and to face challenges with this attitude of Humble Inquiry, becomes especially important for leaders when they recognize their own dependence on the people they are leading.

How Does This Square with Wanting People to Speak Up?

Couldn't we argue that nowadays it is equally important to value *telling*, that people be courageous and tell it like they see it, to speak up to power, to get out of a bystander mentality, to blow the whistle when necessary? The paradox is that the main inhibitor of useful telling is often our own failure to inquire in a way that *makes it safe* for others to tell us the truth, or at least to share all of what they know.

Our failure to ask *humbly* and with the right *attitude* has created work climates in which people do not feel psychologically safe to share what they know. Do we even see such work climates in which people withhold, spin, or even lie because they realize it is not really safe to speak the truth? Or are such "toxic" work climates so commonplace that we fail to even notice this underlying lack of psychological safety?

High-hazard industries, where safety is paramount, especially require reliable communication across hierarchical boundaries. However, we learn from analyses of aviation disasters, chemical/oil industry accidents, nuclear plant incidents, and some NASA missions, that lower-ranking employees had information that may have prevented or lessened negative consequences, but this vital information was either not passed up to higher levels, was ignored, or was over-ridden.

Senior managers often say they are open, that they want to hear from their subordinates, and that they take the information seriously. But when we talk to employees in those same organizations, they tell us they were not asked sincerely, did not feel safe bringing bad news to their bosses even if asked, or tried speaking up but never got any response or acknowledgment. And when we see what happens to whistleblowers, it is a strong signal that truth may be the last thing that some organizations actually want to hear.

We see similar issues in operating rooms, in hospitals, and in the health-care system as a whole. If nurses and technicians do not feel safe bringing contrary information to doctors, whether it's suggesting alternatives or correcting an MD who is about to make a mistake, it is easy to see how patient outcomes can be negatively impacted. Doctors may proclaim that they *do* ask and that their professional environment embraces open flow of relevant information, but if PAs, nurses, and technicians do not feel safe in providing *relevant contextual information,* risks for the patient increase.

Is this the result of employees lacking courage, or is this really the result of leaders and managers not asking humbly? Unfortunately, all too often what is missing is leaderships' recognition that unless they really want to know what is going on, and inquire in a way that convinces others of their open and trusting intent, they will get only responses that their employees think leadership wants to hear. If questions are not posed with Here-and-now Humility, silence, false telling, or spinning may be the more likely and exacerbating response.

Can Humble Inquiry Integrate Competition with Mutual Cooperation and Teamwork?

We know from our responses to disasters and pandemics that we are *all* capable and willing to help each other when help is needed.[2] Yet building relationships between humans is an intricate adaptive process because it requires us to deal simultaneously with our biologically encoded impulses to both compete and cooperate in a cultural context that tends to favor one over the other. In our U.S. culture, it can be especially difficult to build enough trust to feel comfortable asking for help. In addition, when asked for information, others may conceal what they know in order to deceive the "rival" and hence gain power or status.

Because we tout teamwork and like to use lots of different athletic analogies to illustrate it, we use the relay race to illuminate Humble Inquiry and relationship building. To achieve a goal it is often necessary to demonstrate both *superior individual accomplishment* and *effective teamwork*. Winning the race requires not only fast competitive running but also reliable, collaborative baton passing. Reliable baton passing requires open communication and a high level of trust among the runners. We cannot favor one over other, we need both.

Teamwork can become so complicated that it is best compared to a professional U.S. (NFL) football team running an intricate play in which all 11 players have to coordinate their actions with each other as well as react to the opposing team as the play unfolds (or unravels). A surgical team performing a complex procedure needs to coordinate all of the members of the team in real time to even have a chance of coping with unexpected complications. In all of these teamwork cases, can open communication, trust, and coordination develop if members of the team have not built positive relationships with each other through Humble Inquiry?

Humble Inquiry Is about Building Openness and Trust

Building relationships between humans is a biologically intrinsic iterative process, especially in adulthood. We all agree that trusting each other is important, but how do you know, if you need help, that the other person will help? If you need valid information, can you trust others to reveal what they know and not deceive you? Our existing relationships are a tenuous balance easily upset in conversation by withholding or lying. For this reason, Humble Inquiry works only if the attitude behind it includes the desire to really hear what the other person says, to develop an appropriate level of empathy, and to choose a response that shows interest and curiosity. When this process is complemented with situationally appropriate revelations about yourself to others, relationship building—openness and trust—takes off. Humbly inquiring communicates openness, and honestly revealing builds trust. In the pages that follow we hope to convince you why this matters.

READER EXERCISE

In order to actively engage in the Humble Inquiry learning process, we suggest you keep a journal of some kind to record your thoughts as you read. Jot down your reactions, whether you agree or disagree. This learning journal can be a very useful way to bring this material to life as you encounter it, or back to life later, as you work your way through Humble Inquiry and into the Humble Inquiry attitude. Your journal will also be a good place to answer the questions we ask at the end of each chapter. Here's your first one.

Are You Asking in 360 Degrees?

Asking down?
Are you asking and listening to the people who work for you, or are you just telling them what to do? Do you make it safe for those less powerful to speak up to you?

Asking across?
Are you willing to inquire and share with your peers (colleagues or competitors)? Are you willing to show vulnerability to those who share your rank?

Asking up?
Is it safe to raise questions, to inquire for more information or direction from those you work for? Is it safe to speak up or ask up?

1

To Boldly Tell or Humbly Inquire

Conversations go wrong sometimes. Friends, family, and colleagues tell us things we don't want to hear, or they fail to tell us things that would improve matters. We unwittingly offend people by telling them things *they* don't want to hear. Discussions turn into arguments that end in stalemates and hurt feelings. It is critical, now more than ever, to examine what went wrong. If we just let it go, we have a much harder time sorting out later how we can do better with each other the next time we fail to communicate. Can we learn how Humble Inquiry could positively impact our daily conversations, and what can go wrong if it is not used at crucial moments?

Ed's Graudate Student in the MIT Sloan Program

The graduate student was studying for an important finance exam in his basement study. At the family dinner he had explicitly instructed his six-year-old daughter not to interrupt him. He was deep into his work when a knock on the door and a cheery "Hi, Daddy" announced the arrival of his daughter. He said sharply, "I thought I told you not to interrupt me." The little girl burst into tears and ran off. The next morning his wife berated him for upsetting the daughter.

He defended himself vigorously by reminding his wife that he had explicitly told the daughter not to disturb him, until his wife interrupted and said, "I sent her down to you to say goodnight and ask you if you wanted a cup of coffee to help with your studying. Why did you yell at her instead of asking her why she was there?" He did not have any further defense and sank into guilty self-absorption, realizing that he not only had a lot of fence mending to do with both his wife and daughter, but he also began to reflect on a deeper question: why did he yell at his daughter instead of humbly inquiring why she was there? He had to admit to himself that he should have been curious about this violation of his dinnertime order.

If you have ever been in this kind of situation, how could you have done better? The key to Humble Inquiry is to recognize when you need to know why something is happening instead of giving in to a knee-jerk impulse that not only keeps you ignorant but also creates an avoidable disconnect. How can you catch yourself in time to *humbly inquire* what is going on instead of giving in to the impulse of *telling* and assuming that the world will follow your will?

The answer is simple, but its implementation is not. What if you tried these three things: (1) Learn to see, feel, and curb the impulses to lash out; (2) Learn to make a habit of listening and figuring out what is going on *before* taking action; and (3) Try harder to hear, to understand, and acknowledge what others are trying to express to you. What we ask, when we ask it, the particular form in which we ask it, and how we hear and understand the answer—a successful handling of these building blocks will increase the level of trust in our relationships, which, in turn, will reenforce better communication and collaboration.

The husband and wife in this example could revisit this situation with a Humble Inquiry attitude and explore several further questions. Did she really *hear* the intensity of her husband's anxiety about not being interrupted? In that regard, he might well ask, "Why did you send our daughter down instead of coming down yourself?" He might also humbly ask, "Do you understand how anxious I am about this finance stuff and how hard it is for me to concentrate on it?" That might well precipitate an apology from his wife for her punishing morning comment, he might apologize for having lost his cool with the daughter, and the relationship would benefit from the focus on Humble Inquiry in reviewing the situation.

If smoother conversations and comfortable relationships could be achieved by each of us just doing our own thing, all of this might not matter. But if we are on a seesaw (metaphorically speaking) or running a relay race together, it may matter a great deal. Good relationships and open communication are *essential* when all the parties are completely simultaneously interdependent. The baton pass has to work or the race is lost. Recognizing those situations of interdependency then becomes crucial because that is when Humble Inquiry often provides an opportunity that could have easily been missed.

Let's look at an interesting example of how Humble Inquiry might have improved the situation where *telling* was used, and what the Humble Inquiry alternative might have been:

> Jim, the quarterback of a professional U.S. football team, and Rob, his right guard (and therefore the player responsible for protecting him from opposing defensive linemen) are in the locker room after a game.

> **Jim:** Rob, *you* have to do better. I got rushed and
> sacked too many times in today's game.

What struck us about this interaction was not whether
this rebuke in the form of a tell was appropriate, but what
the implications were for the future of this relationship and
the team's performance. It is quite possible that Jim had
every right to give Rob that feedback, and possibly Rob took
it to heart and decided that he would try harder or alter
his technique. Yet from the Humble Inquiry point of view,
they missed a great opportunity that might have gone more
like this.

> **Jim:** Rob, we have to do better. I got rushed and
> sacked too many times in today's game. Any thoughts?
> (Humble Inquiry)
>
> **Rob:** Well I can certainly try harder and adapt to keep
> you better protected, but I need to let you know that
> the team we are playing in two weeks has a defensive
> lineman opposite me who you and I know is a peren-
> nial all-star and may beat me every time. So, on that
> Sunday let's plan for you and the coach to call a differ-
> ent set of plays because I am pretty sure I will have a
> harder time protecting you adequately on that day.
>
> **Jim:** It's great that you pointed this out, lets both
> talk to the coaching staff about it, and work up a
> plan. Thanks.

Had Jim approached Rob with Humble Inquiry, as
in this re-imagining of their conversation, they could
have opened up an important channel of communication
that would not only improve team performance but also
strengthen Jim and Rob's personal relationship, which
might motivate Rob to work out some tactics with Jim that

would benefit Jim's performance. The key to the second version is Jim seeing it as a *we* situation and *asking* Rob what Rob thought about it, which would have communicated to Rob that Jim was genuinely curious and interested in what Rob's solution might be to Jim's getting rushed and sacked so much. The two interdependent players could eventually have built a more personal relationship of the sort that coaches of winning teams often talk about: *teammates who really trust each other.* You only get there if you think in terms of *we.*

Levels of Relationship

To fully understand the relational implications of Humble Inquiry we need to review our model of the *levels of relationship* that are broadly prescribed in our society.

> **Level −1** (domination) is basically a negative relationship characterized primarily by the more powerful telling the less powerful what to do and rejecting efforts to form more equitable relationships.

> **Level 1** relationships are transactional, based on formal role definitions and are characterized by the degree of professional distance that is intentionally maintained between peers (often *competing* peers). In the work setting, the degree of interdependency is prescribed by the formal roles: management is primarily a *telling* process. Humble Inquiry and positive relationship building might be viewed with suspicion or considered irrelevant and inefficient.

> **Level 2** implies getting to know each other at a more personal level in order to develop a higher level of openness and trust, what we refer to as building a

positive relationship. In a conversation, *telling* individuates the parties as teller and listener. Humble Inquiry functions first as an invitation to get closer and more personal and, thereby, enables the sense of *we*, which may then level off and normalize where both parties are comfortable.

In the work setting it will plateau when the team members know each other well enough in relation to their work to be able to handle surprises and complexities. Level 2 relationships offer the promise of flexibility, adaptability, and resiliency, which derive from group members and their leaders learning the gentle art of asking instead of telling.

Level 3 relationships of friendship or love may grow in the more personal and social setting, from a Level 2 relationship, fed by a more consistent Humble Inquiry attitude. People who achieve that level of openness and trust often describe it as really *seeing* each other. This may be thought of as intimacy, and it may actually be entirely appropriate in work settings, provided it does not engender nepotism, favoritism, or other emotionally driven distortions of management decision-making.

TABLE 1.1 Levels of Relationship

Relationship Level	Descriptor
Level –1	Domination/exploitation
Level 1	Transactional (professional distance)
Level 2	Personal (openness and trust)
Level 3	Intimacy

To summarize, *telling* is most consistent with strangers or casual acquaintances chit-chatting, sharing stories, and otherwise transacting in a Level 1 relationship that is based on societal and cultural norms of etiquette, good manners, and tact. As we learn to be more open and trusting, to tell each other what is really going on, we can effectively adapt to new and difficult circumstances. The key is to invite others through Humble Inquiry to move toward a Level 2 relationship.

What Are Some of the Traps in *Telling*?

Many of us experience an everyday work climate in which the preponderance of *telling* can make it very difficult to *ask*, especially to ask in a humble way. Unfortunately, as we noted with Rob and Jim, telling may cut off or preempt the sharing of important information. In addition, telling temporarily puts the other person down. It implies that the other person does not already know what is being told and, by inference, that the other person ought to know it.

We know this feeling well from our own experience of not liking to be told; we generally don't like to be given advice unless we have asked for it. When someone tells you something that you did not ask about, don't you often already know the answer and wonder why the person assumes that you don't? Maybe you even feel offended when you are told things that you already know, are told how to feel about something, or are given unsolicited advice. Didn't Rob already know that he had to do better?

Gratuitous telling betrays three kinds of arrogance: (1) that you think you know more than the person you're telling, (2) that *your* knowledge is the correct knowledge, and (3) that you have the right to structure other people's experience for them. We need to recognize these as traps that we fall into easily and not be surprised or angry if others feel put down. The elderly lady who told Ed about mushrooms not only had incorrect information but also had not been invited to tell Ed anything. Her good intentions to be helpful did not save the situation. The Sloan student who yelled at his little daughter fell into the trap of not knowing why the daughter was there, putting his own needs first, and arrogantly believing that his parental authority was not to be disobeyed. Jim the quarterback fell into a similar trap when he failed to ask Rob for his thoughts on the situation and ideas for possible improvements.

On the other hand, when you genuinely *ask*, you temporarily empower the other person in the conversation and make yourself vulnerable, for a time. You have also opened the door to the possibility of deepening a relationship. The other person may choose to enter the relationship with you but may also belittle you, laugh at you, or in other ways take advantage of you instead of taking you seriously. How you ask the question may also predetermine the direction of the conversation, as is illustrated by this old tale about a traveler and a local (in the days before GPS).

Asking for Directions the Wrong Way

A traveler, on her way to a small town in a rural northern state, stopped at an intersection to ask a local sitting on his porch which of two roads to take.

Traveler: If I take this road, will it lead to Woodford?

Local: Yep, that road will lead you to Woodford.

Traveler: What if I take this other road, will it lead to Woodford?

Local: Yep, that road will also lead you to Woodford.

Traveler: Well, does it make any difference which road I take?

Local: Not to me it don't!

Our traveler assumed the local would care—generally not a bad assumption—but was she ready for the local's indifference? Was the question really Humble Inquiry? Perhaps not. The way she began, "If I take this road," was impersonal and treated the local as just a source of information. Had the traveler said, "I'm looking for the best road to get to Woodford. Can you help me?" *that* might have drawn the local more personally into the situation and displayed a vulnerability that he might not have ignored so easily.

If you don't care about improving communication or building a relationship with the other person, then telling or being impersonal in your questions, as above, may be just fine. But, if some of the goals of the conversation are to improve communication and build a relationship, then it is fair to generalize that telling is less effective than humbly inquiring.

The closed question that comes across as a tell can also be dangerous in leading to misinformation or miscommunication. Asking which road led to Woodford was a *closed question trap* that demanded an answer yet made it harder for the local to reveal what he did or did not know. Perhaps the local had never heard of Woodford or had little patience to engage at all. A closed question may make it much harder for the person being asked the question to concede "I don't know." Worse, it might encourage a casual guess or the withholding of relevant information simply to get the conversation over with.

Successful conversations that lead to productive Level

2 relationships typically start with the assumptions of sociological equity and balance. The wrong kind of tell immediately imbalances the relationship by explicitly or implicitly putting the other person down. If you want to build a relationship, you need to begin by investing something in it. Telling is only an investment if you know for sure that what you are telling is of value to the other person. That is why it is safest to tell only if you have been asked, rather than arrogantly deciding on your own to tell somebody something. It is not unlike when someone chooses to give us feedback—it matters a great deal whether we have asked for it. We only find it really useful when we have asked for it in relation to some goal that we are trying to achieve. You know how you feel when someone says, "Do you mind if I give you some feedback?" There are few among us who are not a bit put off by this because it is not a sincere *ask*; it is a *tell*, and probably contains implicit or explicit criticism. After all, if the feedback is positive, it would probably not be preceded by "Do you mind if..."

Humble Inquiry is an investment in that you are expending some of your *attention* up front, admitting your ignorance, and giving the other person some power. Your questions convey to the other person, "I am prepared to listen to you and am making myself vulnerable to you." You will get a return on your investment if what you learn is something that you did not know before. You will then appreciate that you have been told something new, and a positive relationship can begin to develop through successive cycles of asking and responding in which each of you is *receiving value through what you learn*. In the case of our northern state local, there was a transactional Level 1 exchange, but the value received was not mutual or equal. The relationship had no real basis to develop beyond the one-way exchange.

When there is mutual interest, trust can develop because you have made yourself vulnerable, and the other person has neither taken advantage of you, nor ignored you, nor given you false information. Trust builds for each person because each has shown an interest in and paid attention to what the other person said in response to each question.

> A conversation that builds a trusting Level 2 relationship is, therefore, an interactive process in which *each party invests and gets something of value* in return.

Civility and Here-and-now Humility

All of this occurs within the scripted boundaries of what is considered appropriate good manners and civility in our particular cultural context. Participants exchange information and attention in successive cycles guided by each of their perceptions of the relative cultural boundaries of what it is appropriate to ask and tell in that moment. To fully understand the importance of Humble Inquiry in this cultural context, we need to go back again to the concept of Here-and-now Humility in conversations, relationship building, and task accomplishment. Humility is a very broad concept ranging from its meaning as a character trait to the meaning we wish to emphasize here as a particular feeling in the here-and-now situation. Even the most narcissistic arrogant characters can feel humble in a situation that they cannot understand or control. Even the humblest characters can feel arrogant when they know the answer and are in control of the situation. The trick is not to be preoccupied with personality traits but to learn to read the immediate situation and one's role in it in order to choose wisely when it is important to be here-and-now humble.

To amplify what we said in the introduction, Here-and-now Humility is how you feel when you realize that you are dependent on someone else in the situation. Your status is inferior to the other person at that moment because he or she knows something or can do something that you need in order to accomplish your task or goal. This other person has the power to help or hinder you in the achievement of goals that you are committed to. The traveler who wanted to get to Woodford leaned toward specific questions that only requested *yes* or *no* responses. She did not ask for help; she asked for a judgement on a tell ("Does this road lead...") rather than "Which road..." She got an accurate answer and could have been quickly on her way with the first choice. But that question did not include the possibility that the local had other relevant information and may have been willing to share it.

She did know enough to seek more information, yet again in a second telling manner, she obtained an accurate answer. Did that answer help her make the decision? She did not become aware of her actual dependency for information in this situation. She tried to stay in control with her questions rather than asking for help. The traveler would have been best served if she could access her ignorance and *humbly* ask additional clarifying questions.

Is all this hairsplitting of a trivial example really necessary? Don't we all know how to ask? As the next chapter illustrates, accessing one's own ignorance, or recognizing one's own Here-and-now Humility is not so easy in a culture where we have so many ways of asking that are really *telling* in disguise. You can then either abandon tasks that make you dependent on others or you can deny the dependency, avoid ever feeling humble, fail to get what you need and, thereby, risk failing to accomplish the task. Failing to accept Here-

and-now Humility is often tantamount to effectively sabotaging your own efforts. And people do this all the time. Some would rather risk failure than admit their dependency on someone else. This is as American as rugged individualism.

In Conclusion

As we pointed out in our preface and introduction, the problems we face that are increasingly multifaceted, systemic, fluid, and interdependent will require us to learn how to abandon the less effective Level 1 transactional *telling* modes of adaptation and learn how to insert more expressions of the Humble Inquiry attitude to build the Level 2 relations that will reinforce more adaptive *we* behavior. This is explored in the next chapter.

READER EXERCISE

At this point it would probably help you most to think of examples where things went wrong. For each example, do your own detailed analysis of what you said and how it worked out. If it went badly, reconstruct what might have gone differently, what you could have said instead or at a more appropriate moment. Experiment with alternatives to get a sense of Humble Inquiry and how it differs from telling.

2

The Humble Inquiry Attitude

In the last chapter we described, with some examples of *telling*, how Humble Inquiry relates to levels of relationships. In this chapter we elaborate on the *attitude* of Humble Inquiry as it plays out in different situations. Some of these relationship situations are clearly *Level 2*, but others are not, showing that even in transactional relationships the Humble Inquiry attitude can provide an important invitation to relationship building.

Humble Inquiry is a mix of being helpful, building relationships, and deciphering situations. Thus the most important here-and-now skill for you, the learner, is to build your *situational awareness*. As different situations demand or allow different kinds of behavior, the next most important skill is to develop behavioral *agility* in what you ask, how you ask it, when you ask, when you reveal, and when you display empathy in how you respond. All of these bits and pieces together make up what we think of as the Humble Inquiry *attitude*.

Humble Inquiry as an Attitude

The process of inquiring is both science and art. Professional question askers (pollsters, journalists, social scientists, etc.)

have done decades of research on how to ask a question to get the optimal response. Effective therapists, counselors, coaches, and consultants have refined the art of questioning to a high degree. But most of us typically do not deeply consider how questions should be asked or how to use questions for the many different situations that occur in ordinary conversations.

Humble Inquiry goes beyond mere questioning and displays an attitude of *interest and curiosity* that hopefully engenders a similar reciprocal demeanor of curiosity in the other person in the conversation. You can open the door to a relationship through your own Humble Inquiry, yet a relationship only flourishes if that attitude is reciprocated.

We display this attitude through body language, choice of words, tone, and sometimes even silence, which conveys our patience and curiosity—a way of encouraging the other person to talk. The demeanor and the inquiry signal an effort to see and acknowledge another person in that moment.

My Here-and-now Humility can by itself trigger a very positive and genuine curiosity and interest in you. You will feel acknowledged, and it is precisely my temporary "subordination" that can create *psychological safety* for you, which can increase the chances that you will reveal what I need to know to get a task completed and begin to build our relationship constructively. If you exploit the situation and deceive me, or take advantage of my "subordination" by suggesting something I don't need or is not helpful, I may learn to avoid you in the future, or punish you later if I have the chance or authority. If you tell me what I need to know and help me, we are building a positive Level 2 relationship foundation.

The dilemma in U.S. culture is that we don't really distinguish the construct of Humble Inquiry carefully enough from leading questions, rhetorical questions, direct questions, or statements in the form of questions contrived to be deliberately provocative and intended to put the other person down. If leaders, managers, and all kinds of professionals are to learn Humble Inquiry, they will need to differentiate carefully among the possible questions to ask and emphasize inquiry that builds the relationship rather than just getting to quick answers or quick tells.

Can you build the behavioral muscle memory to ask in a way that builds and consistently reinforces openness and trust? If you are in charge and create the right relationship, you can get answers to the questions you ask. But even more importantly, your Humble Inquiry *attitude* may enable you to also learn answers to the questions *you don't ask* or never thought to ask, and what you learn in those areas may be of far more value in the long run. Jim, our quarterback, is bound to be in much more jeopardy in the upcoming game because he failed to build a closer relationship with Rob, on whom he is dependent. The Humble Inquiry attitude encourages others to broaden the conversation so that you may learn things that you never asked about yet may be very consequential.

Purpose Matters: Do You Know Why You Are There?

Our life is basically a series of situations that we either create, enter into knowingly, or find ourselves drawn into by the actions of others. Learning when to focus on identifying opportunities for Humble Inquiry is akin to becoming *situationally aware*. We need to recognize why we are engaging in a dialogue and what the cultural rules are for a positive conversation.

In any conversation, what are you really trying to do? Perhaps you are seeking information about something you truly do not know or need to know. Your intent might simply be trying to open the door to a constructive relationship. Or you may be trying to show off how smart you are, kill time with chit-chat, convince someone of something, seduce, or give advice.

Your sense of purpose defines your attitude, and knowing why you are in a conversation helps you to clear your head of distractions and irrelevant feelings. An actor friend explained to us how he is able to be present on stage when he has only one line as the butler to introduce the arrival of a new guest. He said, "You have to know *why you are there*, that the whole action of the play depends in some way on your one line." This sounds like a lot of mindfulness for one small line in one small scene. But building the muscle memory to interact this way prepares for bigger acts to follow.

This same principle applies to all our actions in the various situations we act out on our own life stages. When you arrive at your workplace in the morning and enter into various conversations with your colleagues, your manager, and the people who report to you, are you conscious of why you are there that morning? Can you maintain that presence even if your original purpose is to disappear into your cubicle as quickly as you can because you need to jot down some ideas that you had on the way to work?

Developing that inquiring mindset and skill set should make it easier to capitalize on shared moments of inquiry. And rather than keeping that inquiry separate from your own creative purpose, you may discover that your ideas are greatly enhanced by the process of fleshing out new ideas with others.

The Impact of the Humble Inquiry Attitude on Others

An attitude of Humble Inquiry maximizes your curiosity and interest in others and helps to minimize bias and preconceptions about them. It is about training yourself to ask for information in a minimally biased and nonjudgmental way. You do not want to lead others or put them into a position of having to give a scripted socially acceptable response. You want to inquire in a way that maximizes discovery of what is really going on in their context.

This mindset is equally relevant whether you or someone else started the conversation. The potential for a relationship is there, even with a stranger, if either of you wants to start the process of building some kind of connection. Humble Inquiry is therefore most relevant when you find yourself in a conversation that is initially just transactional but develops into something more *personal* because one or both of you want it. The pivotal questions you can ask yourself are, "Do I want to maintain professional distance from this colleague?" or "Do I want to maintain social distance from this personal contact?" If the answer is yes, if professional or social distance is preferred, you may opt not to invest in Humble Inquiry, to remain impersonal and transactional even if the other party opens that door to you by asking you a more personal question. A Level 2 relationship develops only if you both express interest and curiosity in each other.

It is hard to specify whether, when, and how to engage in Humble Inquiry because conversations always occur within variable cultural contexts. If you decide to shift your purpose from being distant to becoming more personal, you probably know how to do that because you will have done it in countless situations before, starting when you first went to school. You will use whatever cues are available in the situation you find yourself in. Generally, and increasingly with younger work populations, underlying Humble Inquiry skills may come even more naturally, reinforced by social and digital tools (particularly chat, voice, and video collaboration). This is not to say that all of us are naturally pure humble inquirers. Some of us find this very easy, others much less so. It is to say that whether at home, in school, or at work, socialization (in modern industrial cultures) provides a basic skill set for all of us, and the key variable is how well we have trained and committed ourselves to tap these skills.

If you are a doctor and have come to believe that you can become a better diagnostician and therapist when you develop closer personal relationships with your patients, you can arrive at your extremely time-constrained full day of appointments with the attitude that the 10 or 15 minutes with each patient may, in fact, be plenty of time to engage with each of them by quickly getting on the same page (particularly about the time constraint itself). Suppose you said, "Sorry the system constrains us so much, but let's make the most of the time we have. What is worrying you?" Many care providers can embrace the effectiveness of creating *we* out of a doctor and patient, such that the time constraint is accepted by both parties, and the patient's issues become even more clearly the focus of information sharing.

This situation may be similar for a manager and a direct report. If you, as the direct report, decide to shift your purpose from being distant to becoming more personal, you will use whatever cues are available in the situation you find yourself in, as Ed unwittingly found out in the following example.

Getting to Know Someone

Ed: When Ken Olsen, the founder of Digital Equipment Corporation, wanted to hire a social psychologist as a consultant, he asked his personal assistant who had come from MIT to find someone. I fit the job profile and was asked to meet with Ken to see whether there would be a good personal chemistry between us.

When I arrived at Ken's office, a large room in an old mill building, I immediately noticed on the walls several canoe paddles and some photographs of woods and streams. Without thinking twice about it, I asked about the canoe paddles on the wall. Ken responded immediately with a detailed account of how every summer he took several weeks off to fly deep into the Canadian woods where he could hike, fish, and totally isolate himself from work.

Ken then asked a few questions about my work at MIT and immediately proposed that I should attend the weekly meeting of the operations committee, which was at that time the governing group of the company. As Ken said, "Just observe us and see if you can help."

Thinking about it afterwards, Ken had invited me into the inner sanctum of the company on virtually no knowledge of who I was, what I did, or whether he could trust me. I concluded that the chemistry between Ken and me was built naturally and quickly, in large part, by my showing a curiosity in his canoe paddles. It seems so trivial, but it was not. This invited Ken to express something he was passionate about and wanted to tell me about, and my listening with interest drew us together personally in a way that shrunk the professional distance very quickly.

Humble Inquiry is best triggered by curiosity and interest wherein a conscious effort is made to minimize controlling or influencing either the content of what the other person has to say, or the form in which it is said. Again, there is a huge difference between open questions and leading questions.

> **Your Humble Inquiry attitude is displayed in how you ask, respond, and reveal yourself to other people.**

The Hidden Power of Humble Inquiry

In our daily life we often find ourselves stuck in disagreements, conflicts, or areas of uncertainty that have not been explored together. Even when you are not in an official helping role, an innocent question (accessing your unfettered ignorance) may clear a logjam with surprising efficiency. So often this is the deepest benefit of having a third party, such as a consultant, who can access ignorance that the first and second parties would not readily admit to. The best kind of leadership may, in fact, be found in well-timed questions from *anyone* rather than the telling of heroic visions or the announcing of brilliant new strategies.

Resolving an Executive Succession Issue

Ed: I was consulting with a large Australian petrochemical conglomerate and was invited to join the senior management team for lunch. In the middle of the lunch, the CEO brought up the news that their VP of Administration was leaving the company. He launched into the issue by announcing that Stuart seemed like a perfectly good candidate to promote but wondered what the other two VPs thought.

The other VPs were clearly nervous about Stuart. They discussed his strengths but somehow continued to feel uncomfortable about him without being able to specify why they were uncomfortable. In effect they were all telling the CEO that Stuart was not right for the job and were framing their objections in the form of vague negative questions about him.

I watched this for a while and became genuinely puzzled why they seemed to like Stuart but could not resolve offering him the job. Curious about what a VP of Admin did in this organization, I asked, "What does the VP of Administration do?"

I got a few impatient and patronizing smiles, but then they condescended to take the time to answer my question: finance, accounting, personnel, long-range planning, and public relations. At this moment one of the VPs said with conviction that it was in public relations that Stuart showed some weaknesses. He was a good inside guy but not effective externally. The other VPs immediately agreed that this was the main reason for their hesitation about offering Stuart the job.

And then one of them asked, "Does PR have to be part of this job? In fact, with all the new environmental laws in Australia being such an issue, shouldn't we have a full-time Sr. VP dedicated solely to PR?" The group agreed immediately to separate out PR, search for someone to fill that role, and promote Stuart, who was perfect for the remaining internally-focused administrative leadership functions.

I learned from this that the best approach is to access my ignorance, allow my curiosity to lead me, and to ask innocent questions. (What does the VP of Admin do?) Accepting and revealing one's ignorance can be very powerful in opening up the dialogue, freeing the logjam, and, in this case, clarifying a crucial succession problem.

Another quite different example suggests how a powerful executive can tap his own Here-and-now Humility by accessing his own ignorance and curiosity in a way that empowers his employees.

Inquiry across Hierarchy

DEC CEO Ken Olsen used to wander around the company, stop at an engineer's desk and ask, "What are you working on?" Ken was able to convey that he was not checking up on people but was genuinely interested. He and an engineer could end up in a long conversation that would be technically and personally satisfying for both of them. Even when the company had over 100,000 people worldwide, Ken was well known and loved by DEC employees because so many had experienced him as a humble inquirer in this manner. This affection was especially surprising because Ken could also be brutal and tyrannical at times when his senior managers disappointed him by not treating their employees with the same Humble Inquiry attitude. The quickest way to spark Ken's displeasure was a lack of Here-and-now Humility in any of his engineers and managers.

Ken was a great example of how someone in a very senior position can get to know even the lowest-status members of an organization if the purpose is to build relationships rather than measure, control, or judge. Hard as it was for junior engineers to believe that Ken was actually ignorant about what they were doing—and was genuinely curious—they appreciated being treated as *adults* worthy of personal relationships, regardless of rank or reporting structure.

Humble Inquiry has the potential to humanize relationships across hierarchical and geographical boundaries, especially when people reveal aspects of themselves that are relatable. Of course each person's experiences are unique. Yet the events of any story we tell reveal how we perceive things, feel about them, and act on them, which sooner or later provides opportunities for empathizing. Ideally, inquirers remember something similar from their own experiences and can identify with the storyteller. When we share our stories, we provide each other opportunities to discover important similarities in our experiences and our reactions, even as we know that experiences still differ in many ways. We have to listen and understand—this allows us to identify with the storyteller, which in turn prompts us to inquire further. Humble Inquiry helps build trust rather than turning the dialogue toward yourself. It means staying "on your own side of the net" as a listener until you are invited over to the other side or feel confident that you have something important and helpful to add.

Does Humble Inquiry Have to Be Sincere?

Can we simulate interest and get credit for caring if we do not have the attitude and the constructive motive? Humans are very sensitive, with highly tuned emotional radars. We also may be better at perceiving insincerity in others than we are in hiding the mixed signals we send out to others. An insincere boss is spotted quickly and often resented. Faux humility comes across loud and clear. Generally, no matter how you phrase your questions, others will sense it immediately if you are not at all interested in them. At the same time, if the attitude behind the behavior is correctly perceived to be sincere interest, even some kinds of *telling* may have the same positive effect as Humble Inquiry.

In Conclusion

The best way to close this chapter is to remind ourselves that Humble Inquiry is, in the end, both an attitude and a conversational tactic, something that you know how to do, have probably chosen to do many times when you were interested in building a relationship, and can use both in your work and social life in situations that need a reset or realignment. It is therefore best thought of not as a communication formula but as a nuanced behavior pattern that has applications in a wide variety of situations.

Think about a time you realized how Here-and-now Humility helped you uncover information that led you to build a more positive open Level 2 relationship with another person. Can you envision different approaches to difficult conversations, such as back-and-forth debates that are full of conflict, where what is needed is the humble question that defuses the conflict or clarifies the issue? In the previous chapter we illustrated how this might work with the graduate student father who yelled at his daughter, and the quarterback who failed to see his dependence on his right guard.

When Humble Inquiry unblocks and clarifies—enabling conversations to progress—we see it, and we learn.

It enables us to be helpful even when that is not our primary purpose. If your purpose is specifically to be helpful in a mentoring, coaching or counseling role, what might you do differently? To sharpen the distinction between Humble Inquiry and the kind of inquiry that is specifically used by therapists, coaches, and counselors, we explore those other forms, and how they overlap, in the next chapter.

READER EXERCISE

This chapter might have triggered memories of times when you intervened constructively or used Humble Inquiry as part of building a relationship. Use these personal examples or build on the ones you identified after Chapter 1 to respond to the following questions in your journal:

- What triggered you to intervene in a Humble Inquiry manner?

- What exactly did you do? What words did you use? What attitude did you display?

- What were the positive (or negative) expected (or unexpected) consequences?

- What have you learned so far?

The purpose of this self-analysis is to become acquainted with your own skills, your own barriers, and your needs to unlearn old habits and learn new skills.

3

How Is Humble Inquiry Different?

One of the best ways to understand Humble Inquiry is to position it relative to some other forms of inquiry. We have a tendency to think of asking or telling as just simple alternatives when, in fact, there are many forms of each with different consequences. In the last chapter we took a deep dive into the essential elements of Humble Inquiry that can play important roles in many kinds of situations. In this chapter we cover the kind of inquiry used by designated helpers, such as teachers, coaches, counselors, and therapists.

To begin, a basic difference lies in the purpose. We see Humble Inquiry as primarily about reducing one's ignorance, making sense of complicated situations, and in that process, deepening relationships. In contrast, the primary role of *helping* inquiry is to *influence*—to teach, coach, counsel, and heal. We often see Humble Inquiry used at the early stages of helping because deepening a relationship is also crucial in the helping process; but the reverse—using Humble Inquiry to deliberately control another person—is usually identified quickly as insincere and, therefore, may backfire.

Forms of Inquiry in Helping a Client

Helping inquiry is used to influence, but because the helper also wants to learn as much as possible about the client in order to establish an open and trusting Level 2 relationship, helpers may find that the best way to start is with Humble Inquiry. As the client's concerns are revealed, the helper can shift toward three other forms of inquiry:

Diagnostic inquiry steers the client's thought process and conversation toward areas that the helper considers to be relevant to providing help.

Confrontive inquiry not only influences the direction of the conversation but adds the helper's own ideas, concepts, or advice as part of the question. Each type of inquiry influences the client to a different degree and in different ways.

Process-oriented inquiry invites the client to examine the actual helping process itself so that both helper and client can assess whether help is being delivered or not.

DIAGNOSTIC INQUIRY

One of the most common alternatives to Humble Inquiry occurs when you get curious about a particular thing the other person is telling you and *you* choose to focus on it. You are not *telling* with this kind of question, but you are *steering* the conversation and influencing the other person's attention toward what *you* are curious about, and you may be indifferent at that moment to the possible impact on the other person. This was illustrated in the last chapter with the example of Ed asking in the middle of the conversation, "What does the VP of Administration do?" It may be seen there as an example of Humble Inquiry because Ed was truly ignorant and was clearly not trying to be a consultant. But the impatient, condescending answer Ed received clearly illustrated the point that this kind of question can be an interruption and seen as a takeover by the person doing the asking.

By asking a *diagnostic* question instead of continuing to encourage the unfolding of the client's story, you are taking charge of the direction of the conversation and should, therefore, consider whether or not this is desirable. The main issue is whether this steering is in the interest of actual problem-solving and helping, or simply indulging your curiosity in a way that may not be helpful. The worst examples of unhelpful diagnostic inquiry are what reporters do to elicit something "newsworthy," what lawyers do to witnesses to elicit information that is just favorable to their position, what sales people do to sell customers what they may not need, what debaters do to trap their opponents into taking untenable positions, and what interrogators do to get confessions.

There are three types of diagnostic questions: ones looking to make sense of the situation, ones that elicit emotional reactions, and ones trying to find out what actions have been—or need to be—taken. These questions can be thought of as different kinds of interventions to help decipher the context in which a client is operating.

Making Sense of the Situation

When helpers ask, "Why do you suppose that happened?" they are asking about motivation or causes, which may focus clients on their own thought processes or purposes. As innocent and supportive as these questions might seem, they do take the floor away temporarily, can impose control on the situation, and may cause the client to think about something that may not be entirely relevant to the problem or task at hand.

Emotional Reactions

"How did (do) you *feel* about that?" This question is different from Humble Inquiry because asking for feelings may be pushing deeper than the other is willing to go. Asking about feelings is one way to become more personal in the relationship, which may be appropriate in the helping situation and can also feel like the right empathic direction to take in Humble Inquiry. The risk is that it may also be jumping the gun. Not everyone is prepared to talk about their feelings or even know what they are.

Actions Taken or Contemplated

"What have you done about this?" and "What are you going to *do* next?" are action-oriented questions clearly designed to push others to focus on what they did or plan to do in the future. This line of questioning can be helpful and overlaps with Humble Inquiry, as illustrated in the following example that also includes confrontive inquiry, reflecting what the helper thinks should be done.

An Invitation to Study an Organizational Culture

Ed received a call from the head of organization development (OD) of a large power utility inquiring whether he would be willing to do a culture analysis of their organization. Ed inquired whether it was the CEO who had made this request in order to find out if the commitment to change was serious. To test this further Ed asked whether the CEO would be willing to meet at his home because showing up at the client organization would be an intervention with unknown consequences that neither party would be ready to deal with at that early stage. The CEO agreed and they met at Ed's home some weeks later with his COO and the head of OD, who was the project manager for this culture change initiative. The following dialogue occurred in a relaxed setting in Ed's garden.

Ed: (Initiating with Humble Inquiry) So can you tell me a bit about what is going on?

CEO: Our problem is that we are a very old company and now have a very rigid and stodgy culture. We need to change the culture in order to be relevant to current times.

Ed: Can you give me an example of what you mean by an old stodgy culture? (Humble Inquiry)

At this point the COO, who had been with the company for about a year and was hired partly to bring about changes, jumped into the conversation.

COO: I can give you a perfect example that just happened to me yesterday. I have created a task force of 15 people with whom I meet every few weeks to make change plans. We have a big circular room and, as so often happens in groups, each person sits in the same seat at every meeting. Yesterday only five people showed up, and guess what? Even though this forced them to sit very far from each other, they sat in the same seats that they always do. I was astonished at this rigid behavior, and that's a great example of what we mean by being stuck with the stodgy culture and why we need your help in figuring out how to assess further and develop a change process.

Ed: I'm astonished as well. So what did you do? (Diagnostic inquiry)

After a long pause, the COO blurted out, "Oh wow—I didn't do anything!"

After another long pause, all four of us experienced a collective moment of great insight.

CEO: What you just said, that you didn't do anything, made me realize that we don't need an outside assessment. We just need to begin to act on those behaviors that we observe that no longer make any sense. We have allowed and maybe even encouraged some of the old rituals that we are now calling stodgy. We now need to change our *own behavior* to signal that many of the old ways of doing things will no longer work. So, with Ed's help, let's figure out when we personally have condoned what we don't like, and in what way we could behave differently in the future.

This led to a very constructive discussion and the setting of some goals, with plans to reconvene virtually in a couple of weeks to share their experiences of what changes had occurred. We had several such virtual discussions in the next few months, and Ed learned that they had made great progress in communicating what new behavior they would expect, reinforce, and reward.

Ed had no idea when he impulsively asked his diagnostic question that it would be so impactful in enabling them to break out of their own inertia. In some way they had forgotten or never realized that it is the formal leaders who communicate new ways of doing things and have many levers for embedding new values in new behavioral norms. They did not need to study the culture—they needed to change their own behavior and, thereby, communicate what changes needed to be made. At the same time, we need to note that it was the earlier Humble Inquiry question, "Can you give me an example?" that led to the productive diagnostic question, "What did you do?"

Systemic Questions Regarding the Total Situation

Helpers exploring the client's story will hear about other actors in the story and about their interdependencies. They will identify the roles played by the client's family, friends, bosses, colleagues, and others in this whole complex system. If they are helping clients to better understand the systems they live in, they may need to ask them how others in that system think, feel, and act. Considering different perspectives often then leads to important reframing of the content that the client is presenting, which is a crucial element of sense making and, therefore, also integral to Humble Inquiry. The following questions may be useful in prompting clients to look at their situations from other points of view.

"What do you think *they* were thinking about this?" (Sense making)

"How do you think *the group* felt about this?" (Emotional responses)

"What did *she (he, they)* do then?" (Actions taken)

The importance of understanding the whole system is illustrated in the next example in which a manager found himself adopting a helping role.

The Responsible Electrical Worker and Helpful Boss

A large urban energy utility had very firm rules about wearing protective equipment, such as face shields. On a routine inspection it was discovered that a worker had lifted his shield and thereby exposed his face and eyes to danger. He was immediately terminated, but the manager conducted a mandatory review.

Manager: What were you thinking? You know the rules, and you know you were risking your eyes to some kind of flash. Can you tell me the whole story of what happened that day? (Telling, then Humble Inquiry)

Employee: I went down into the underground service unit and started to fix the equipment when my shield suddenly fogged up completely, because it was a very hot and humid day, and I literally could not see just at the moment when I had to finish the splice.

Manager: Don't we have anti-fogging eye-shields for this kind of weather? (Diagnostic inquiry)

Employee: No, we only have one type and it clearly does not work well on this kind of day.

Manager: Wasn't there someone else with you who could have helped? (Systemic question)

Employee: Yes, and he had exactly the same problem, could not see, so the only thing I could do to finish the job was to lift my shield...

As a result of this revelation, the employee, who had an excellent safety record in all other respects, was not only reinstated but was asked to become a member of an ad hoc task force whose tasks were to find a supplier that sold safety shields that would not fog up in humid weather and to recommend to headquarters that these safety shields be provided to all service unit workers. The systemic exploration revealed something that apparently either had not been noticed by the company or had been dismissed as too expensive.

The manager in this case may have seemed accusatory by beginning with "What were you thinking?" Yet it worked in this situation because the employee could tell, from the questions that followed, that the manager was sympathetic, and not out to accuse the employee of a violation. The manager was sincere in the most important question, "Can you tell me the whole story of what happened that day?" This communicated mutual fact-finding—not punishment. The questions were diagnostic, but the *attitude* was Humble Inquiry, and both parties understood that, once the manager got to the open diagnostic question. Whether such questions can be thought of as Humble Inquiry then depends on the tone and context in which they are asked and on the state of the relationship between the two parties.

CONFRONTIVE INQUIRY

Confrontive inquiry is different from diagnostic inquiry in that helpers intentionally insert *their own ideas* in the form of a question. The question may still be based on curiosity or interest, but it is connected to the helper's *own ideas* of what could or should happen next. Confrontive inquiry is in pursuit of information related to something that you, as the helper, want or that you are thinking about. You have crossed over the net, and it becomes about *you* as much or more than the client.

Almost by definition this form of inquiry can rarely be thought of as Humble Inquiry because the inquirer is taking charge of both the process and content of the conversation. Tacitly giving advice often arouses resistance and makes it harder to build the Level 2 relationship, because others are put in a position where they feel they have to explain or defend themselves.

Confrontive questions can occasionally communicate

the attitude of Humble Inquiry if the motive is to be helpful and if the relationship has sufficient trust established
to allow the other to feel helped rather than confronted.
Timing, tone of voice, and various other cues signal your
purpose. What is most important is to first *confront yourself*
with the question of what your purpose is before you ask a
confrontive question. Are you feeling curious, or have you
fallen into thinking you have an answer and are just testing
out whether or not you are right? If you are just testing your
own ideas, then you have drifted into *telling* and it should not
be surprising if the other person gets defensive.

The negative consequences of this form of questioning
can be much more serious if the questioner is not clear about
his or her own purpose, as illustrated in the next example.

The Canning-line Problem and the Confrontive Boss

Mark, a young college graduate in mechanical engi-
neering, decided to enter an elite year-long management training program in a major international
packaged-foods company. After graduating from the
program, Mark was sent to a fruit-canning plant in
Montana to take over a 15-person crew that ran a
large canning line. Mark was an easy-going, friendly
person who established good personal relationships
with his older unionized canning-line crew.

Unfortunately, they were working with an old canning
machine that periodically broke down and required
repairs that often took so much time that the crew
would miss production targets. On those missed tar-
get occasions, Mark's supervisor immediately called
Mark in and demanded to know who screwed up this
time and who should be fired (confrontive questions).

Mark explained in clear rational terms that the machine was aging and simply needed to be repaired periodically, requiring halting the line and making some fixes. But Mark's supervisor was convinced that there was always an individual who failed to do something correctly and therefore needed to be identified and disciplined. Nothing Mark said changed the boss's assumption, and Mark came to realize that the same assumptions characterized most of the other managers in this organization. It was deeply embedded in the managerial culture that one always solved problems by finding someone to blame, which led Mark to leave the company after a year. The underlying problem was management's inability to hear—not the aging machine or Mark and the crew.

This case highlights what can happen when the person doing the confronting cannot listen to the reaction of the person being confronted. In stark contrast to the supervisor at the electric power utility, Mark's supervisor was *telling* not *inquiring*. He was accusing, not problem-solving, regardless of how he posed the questions. Had the canning-line supervisor used Humble Inquiry, or even diagnostic inquiry, the organization might have learned that it needed to start planning to replace that canning-line machinery. Instead, they had to replace a talented engineer who found no good reason to stay with a confrontive—if not irrational—management team.

Where helpers differ most from humble inquirers is in the use of *diagnostic* or *confrontive inquiry,* so we will highlight (in Table 3.1) this difference before discussing *process-oriented inquiry.*

TABLE 3.1   Diagnostic versus Confrontive Inquiry

	Diagnostic Inquiry	Confrontive Inquiry
Sense making	Why do you suppose they were acting that way?	Were they acting that way because they were scared?
Feelings	How did that make you feel?	Didn't that make you angry?
Action-oriented	What did you do?	Why didn't you say something about it?
Systemic	How were the others in the room reacting?	Were the others in the room surprised?

PROCESS-ORIENTED INQUIRY

An option that is always on the table is to shift the conversational focus onto the conversation itself. Whether this moves the conversation toward Humble Inquiry or not depends on the purpose of the person shifting the focus. If you are trying to develop a good relationship and feel the conversation starting to go in the wrong direction, you can humbly ask some version of "Are we OK?" "Is this working?" or "What is happening here?" to explore what might be going wrong and how it might be improved.

Instead of continuing with the *content* of the conversation, this kind of inquiry suddenly focuses on the context, on the *interaction* itself. How such a process question might be worded depends very much on the actual situation. Generally, it should have the effect of making the other person (client) aware that *these interaction dynamics* can be reviewed and analyzed. If the goal is Humble Inquiry and you feel that it is not working, consider these types of questions:

■ Are we getting anywhere?
■ What do you think is happening between us right now?

- Have we gone too far?
- Am I offending you?
- Are we getting too personal?

Process-oriented inquiry itself can also be thought of as diagnostic (Why did you choose to tell me about the problem in this particular way?), confrontive (Why were you so defensive just now when I was trying to tell you how I felt?), or systemic (Have I gotten us too far off what you were trying to tell me by asking about all these other people?).

The power of this kind of inquiry is that it focuses on the relationship and enables both parties to assess whether their relationship goals are being met. Used with Here-and-now Humility, this kind of inquiry is probably also the most difficult to learn because our culture may not view this as constructive or productive conversation. We are driven to get things done, to problem solve—not to stop progress to ask how we are feeling or how we are doing. Still, this form of inquiry is often the most powerful way to get out of awkward or difficult conversations because it allows both parties to reset, to restate what they are there for, what they want, and, in other ways, recalibrate and restate their expectations. Such resets are especially important when we feel that conversations have somehow gone wrong in a relationship that both parties want to deepen. In those instances, process-oriented inquiry can be usefully launched at a later time when the emotions aroused in the conversation have cooled down. In the example in Chapter 1—in which the MIT graduate student yells at his daughter—such process-oriented inquiry was crucial in reestablishing the family harmony.

> **What you ask, the content of the question defines the situation.**

In Conclusion

We have now explored various forms of asking and telling. Just saying to yourself that you should ask more and tell less does not by itself build positive Level 2 relationships of openness and mutual trust; nor does it fulfill the purpose of being helpful. Humble Inquiry starts with the attitude and is then supported by our choice of questions. The more we remain curious about the other person in the current context—before letting our own expectations and preconceptions creep in—the better our chances are of staying in the right questioning mode. The more we take a collaborative helping purpose into our conversations, the more likely we are to improve the relationship. Showing off, for example trying to tell an even better joke than the other person, is more likely to cause damage. Your best bet is to blend the various forms of helping inquiry with Humble Inquiry, according to the needs of the situation.

We have to learn that diagnostic and confrontive questions come very naturally and easily, just as telling comes naturally and easily. It takes some discipline and practice to access your ignorance and stay focused, at least initially, on the other person through Humble Inquiry. As we get into conversations and as mutual openness and trust build up, bouncing back and forth between Humble Inquiry and the various forms of diagnostic, confrontive, and process-oriented inquiry can often blend effectively with each other, but it is important to be conscious of when you are switching from one kind of inquiry to another.

If we learn to do this, the positive consequences should be better conversations and better relationships. For many situations it may not matter, or we may not care. But especially if you are dependent on others, if you are the person in charge trying to increase the likelihood that your colleagues will help you and be open with you, Humble Inquiry used at the right time can open the door to vital information exchange.

READER EXERCISE

You have now read about when and how Humble Inquiry comes into play and how it connects with other forms of inquiry. Review what you have learned about your own successes in using forms of inquiry in building relationships and deciphering complex situations.

Can you identify and classify the successful incidents and contrast them with unsuccessful ones? This analysis will give you your own experience base to investigate as we move into some of the reasons why Humble Inquiry is not as natural as we might like it to be.

The final section of this book offers a series of exercises that further explore these distinctions between forms of inquiry; it may be interesting at this juncture to practice with these exercises.

4
The Culture of Do and Tell

A critical enabler or inhibitor of Humble Inquiry is the culture in which we grew up, live, and work. The U.S. macroculture frames our views on living, loving, working, and dying. We work in a technical culture that may be driven largely by our professions, our occupations, our industries, and our markets. And we live *and* work in a social culture that reinforces and adapts to our macrocultural norms and creates for us the roles and rules of daily social life, what we end up calling "good manners," "tact," and "etiquette."

When we observe our culture, and analyze it with some detachment or objectivity, we can describe language, art, design, and social conventions as "artifacts." The artifacts of a culture also include the daily behavior that we see, hear, and otherwise experience. However, artifacts are not as easy to decipher as they are to see and hear, so we have to talk to people and ask them questions about what things mean. When we pose questions about U.S. culture, we elicit espoused values such as freedom, equality of opportunity, individual rights, and other values that we may even refer to as "our constitutional rights."

When we compare some of the artifacts and behaviors that we observe with some of the espoused values, we often find inconsistencies, which signal a deeper level to culture that consists of tacit assumptions. Such assumptions may have been new or aspirational values at one time, and, as we learned that the behaviors inspired by those values helped the United States to survive and grow, they became embedded and eventually taken for granted and non-negotiable. It is these tacit assumptions that really drive our manifest behavior and *define much of our reality.*

An interesting example of this in the United States is that we claim to value teamwork and tell our organization members "you should be team players," yet our promotional and reward systems are almost entirely individualistic and competitive. We espouse equality of opportunity and freedom, but the reality of poorer educational opportunities and various forms of unconscious bias against minority populations suggest that there may be deeper tacit assumptions based on "rugged individualism" and "self-determination" that operate at the same time and deeply influence our behavior.

Tacit assumptions that underlie a given culture may or may not be congruent with each other. For example, with regard to linear straightforward tasks, we promote individualistic competitive behavior, but when tasks are complex and require collaboration, we espouse teamwork. Underlying this seeming inconsistency is the deeper assumption of *pragmatism.* We are task oriented and promote the values and methods *that work.* Not unlike other cultures, U.S. culture can flourish with inconsistencies and internal conflicts because in a constantly changing physical and social context, pragmatism can turn into effective adaptation and agility. With respect to values such as humility, debating whether or not it is an important personality trait becomes irrelevant so long as we understand that our concept of Here-and-now Humility is a crucial skill for effective adaptation.

Generally, cultures have rules about rank and respect based on deep assumptions about what defines status. In many societies, basic humility toward persons whose positions are based on birthright is taken for granted. In more egalitarian and individualistic societies, we tend to respect high achievers, self-made go-getters, even rebels and revolutionaries. We may feel a sense of comparative humility in the presence of those who have achieved more, those who really get stuff done. However, mutual Here-and-now Humility is often missing because we don't even recognize our interdependency.

Valuing Task Outcomes over Relationship Building

Let's dig a little deeper into some observations about U.S. culture: We generally believe that the basic unit of society is the individual, whose rights should be protected. We are entrepreneurial and admire individual accomplishment. We thrive on competition. Optimism and pragmatism show up in the way we are oriented toward the short term and in our ambivalence about long-range planning. We prefer to run things until they break because we believe we can then fix them or replace them. We might be accused of can-do arrogance since, deep down, we believe we can fix anything, as illustrated in the adage "*Impossible* just means it takes a little longer."

Some cultures consider relationships to be intrinsic to getting the job done and deliberately spend time building trust. In the United States, faced with relationship-building activities, we often get impatient and would rather get to work. And now with information technology's ability to speed up virtually everything, we may be even more impatient. Most important of all, we see in all dimensions of

U.S. culture a strong bias to over-value task accomplishment relative to relationship building, and we are either unaware of this cultural bias or, worse, indifferent to it. Why bother fixing how we build relationships when it is not clear that anything is broken?

Related to this individualistic task bias is the vague sense that we do not really like or trust groups. All too often we see committees and meetings as time we will never get back, partly because we assume that group decisions diffuse accountability when what we favor is individual account-ability. We spend money and time on team building only when it appears to be pragmatically necessary to get the job done. We publicly tout teamwork and congratulate the win-ning team (an espoused value), but we generally don't believe that the team could have done it without the individual star, who usually receives the greatest reward.

Sometimes we just don't clearly see where teamwork is essential. In the Summer Olympic games, the United States usually has some of the world's fastest runners yet has lost some high-profile relay races because we failed to pass the baton effectively. Individually the relay teammates may be great stars, but is it okay if collectively they fail in the team's task? We assign accountability to the individual; we look for someone to praise for victory and someone to blame for de-feat. The individual is where "the buck stops."

Instead of genuinely valuing relationships and good teamwork, we often admire individual competitiveness, such as outdoing each other conversationally, pulling the clever con game, and even selling "benefits" that a customer may not need. We generally do not question our belief in *caveat emptor* (let the buyer beware). "There's a sucker born every minute" is a whimsical justification for competitive-ness. We value our freedom without explicitly acknowledging that this breeds competitiveness as well as caution and mistrust of each other.

In many U.S. companies we have seen how status and prestige are associated with a track record of task accomplishment. Once a high achiever has elevated status above others, it is common for the high achiever to feel entitled to start telling others what to do, regardless of formal rank ascension. The best engineers and the best sales executives are often promoted to supervisor roles where they can direct others what to do. Compensation, and its public display, is a common proxy for status, reinforced by some pay scales that determine managers' income based on how many subordinates they have on their "team."

Technology companies have developed parallel career ladders (shadow hierarchies) for technical experts with special skills and contributions to their fields. It is not necessarily the case, however, that these parallel hierarchies offer parallel compensation to the formal management hierarchy. All of this adds up to an individualistic, transactional bias to getting it done and getting ahead. For this and other reasons, professional distance across rank levels is considered okay if not preferred. In fact, personal relationships across ranks may be considered perilous if such relationships lead to implicit bias in assigning work and rewards (which would violate our meritocratic espoused values about egalitarian order).

In modern U.S. health-care systems, we vocally deplore the fact that the system limits the amount of time that doctors can spend with patients because of our espoused value that building a relationship with patients is good medicine. But we accept the necessity for short doctor–patient visits as inevitable because at some level we accept the deeper tacit assumption that economic criteria rather than social benefits should undergird the system. We accept what we regard as economic necessities even though there is growing evidence that communication problems between doctors and patients cause treatment failures. All of this is driven by the need to accomplish tasks in a cost-effective manner, which translates into cramming as many tasks as possible into each unit of time and not prioritizing relationship building because it might take too long or cost too much.

Our apologies if this seems like a harsh view of U.S. management culture. There are certainly trends in other directions, but when we deal with culture at the tacit-assumption level, we have to think clearly about what many of our current assumptions really are, quite apart from our espoused values reflecting more humanistic intentions. The result of a pragmatic, individualistic, competitive, task-oriented culture is that humility, in its common conception, is relatively low on the work/productivity value scale, and Humble Inquiry is not a spontaneous impulse.

When a Culture Favors Telling over Asking

How often do we take it for granted that telling is more appropriate than asking? Asking the right questions is valued, while asking in general is not. Even further, asking the *right question* may actually mean inquiry is being cleverly used to trigger efficient task accomplishment. To ask out of ignorance is to reveal weakness, isn't it? Expert knowledge is highly valued, hence telling people what we know is almost automatic. (We are reminded of the quip, "Wow, he really knows a lot, and sometimes he's even right.") We are especially prone to telling when we have been empowered by someone else's question or when we have been formally promoted into a position of power (formal authority).

Ed once asked a group of management students what it meant to them to be promoted to manager. They all said without hesitation, "It means I can now tell others what to do."

Of course, the dangerous hidden assumption in that dictum is that once people are promoted, they will then magically *know* what to do. The idea that the manager might come to a direct report and ask, "What should we do?" would be considered abdication, a show of weakness, a failure to fulfill the leadership role. If you are a manager or a leader, you are supposed to know what to do, or at least *appear* to know what to do.

Telling (in this case, a management direction) is not only expected and respected, it also feels good when we think we have solved someone else's problem. What could be more satisfying than being asked to give advice? And how easy is it for us to assume that our feedback or advice will be valued? Offering feedback comes easily to many of us, especially for those in supervisory positions, and it is only later that we discover that our advice was ignored rather than valued, and possibly even deemed offensive.

Many of us also work in a professional context resembling what Stephen Potter some time ago described as *gamesmanship*, *one-upmanship*, and *lifemanship*.[3] This was British humor at its best, but it was a much deeper commentary on how Western culture values competition, even in conversation. Potter noted that there are several ways to gain points in competitive conversation: making a smart remark, putting down someone who has claimed too much, and turning a clever phrase even if it embarrasses someone else in a conversation. We compete on who can tell the *most*—the most interesting story, the most outrageous adventure, or the best joke.

Of course, outdoing someone else is only good if it is done within the cultural bounds of proper etiquette. Embarrassing or humiliating someone in the conversation is generally not okay, and, if one consistently does this, one may end up socially ostracized. In the United States, in particular, we are becoming less and less tolerant of verbal bullies. To be an effective gamesman, Potter noted in the subtitle of *Gamesmanship,* one must know "how to win without actually cheating." Or, to be effective in *Lifemanship,* he provides the subtitle that it is "the art of getting away with it without being an absolute plonk."

One implication in all of this is that, deep down, many in the United States share a zero-sum mindset that if we are not winning, we are losing. If you don't tell first, someone else will tell and get the recognition and take the lead. If you are not leading, you are following. Don't we always seek out an alpha who will do and not dither? The ideal of reciprocal cooperation where both parties win is rarely our shared goal except where absolutely necessary.

We also know how important telling is from our desire in most conversations to get to the point. When we are listening to someone and don't see where it is going, we ask, "So what is your point?" We expect conversations to get to a conclusion, which is reached by *telling* something, not by asking more open-ended questions. Telling preserves our linearity; too many questions just sidetrack or circle back. When we are in the telling mode, we hope to direct, to impress, to score points, to entertain. When we are in the questioning and listening mode, we welcome being guided, impressed, entertained, even distracted, yet this mode may be viewed as too passive and not to be associated with task achievement.

Our colleague Lotte Bailyn has noted how much this view of work also fits the traditional stereotype of the alpha male, whose tendency is to tell, which leads us to question whether these values create and reinforce glass ceilings for women in organizations.[4] Would the culture of management evolve if more women made it to senior positions with stronger biases toward Humble Inquiry, reducing professional distance and building Level 2 personal relationships across hierarchical levels?

In any case, as we noted in Chapter 1, there is a problem with telling and an associated trap that we must be aware of, as is illustrated in the following example.

Short-term Gain, long-term Harm?

Pat was a product manager at a technology company in the mid-1990s, in the early days of the World Wide Web. The company was going strong, with new technology being developed and introduced to new markets at an impressive clip. Pat was leading a strategy for a product that was equal parts software and information. As such, there were two principal product leaders—Pat for software, and Chris for information content. While somewhat artificial, this split (in fact symbiosis) allowed the organization to follow parallel development tracks while keeping things tightly synchronized. All parties had their domains of expertise, and all were on the same overall product team.

In a product-planning meeting, the team came to a logjam; decisions needed to be made and there was a sense of drifting into vague dithering. Pat decided this was one of those moments of truth that needed bold direction setting to (a) signal grit and authority and (b) maintain momentum for the team at large.

Pat: Alright, here's what we will do ... (A decisive tell)

The group responded: a few advocates of the idea agreed and chimed in, followed by a quick show of hands, for and against. This yielded a quorum and a majority, so that the overall group could go on, decision made, logjam cleared, alignment accomplished. This brought the meeting back on track, post impasse, and on to the next important milestone.

Later that day, Chris, who had remained poker-faced during the meeting, confronted Pat.

Chris: What was that all about?

Pat was a bit surprised, feeling the group had made good progress.

Chris: It's not up to you to declare "Here's what we will do." (Confrontive tell)

Chris explained that Pat, as a peer and partner, went too far in asserting leadership by proclaiming "Here's what we *will* do," not even suggesting what the team "could" or even "should" do. In that jointly led meeting among interdependent peers, it was no one individual's place to declare we "will."

That said, Pat was acting in line with U.S. management norms of decisiveness and seizing de facto authority, as all great leaders are called on to do in times of dithering indecision. Chris, on the other hand, was expressing completely justified frustration—if not anger—that one individual's "will" captured the moment and led the team in an unvetted direction, and, at the same time, may have created an illusion that Pat was the alpha, or *real* boss, of this group, something that was not true and that Chris objected to strongly.

Why was this a problem? The problem is that in the culture of do and tell, word choices are often normalized by management conventions and fail to call out trivial but very powerful oversteps such as "here's what we *will* do." Pat may well have felt that using an equivocation like "could" or "should" would weaken the leadership assertion. And asking the group how they would feel about several possible directions would be virtually unthinkable in this hard-driving climate. Unfortunately, however, using the term "will" yielded the unintended consequence of creating (not eliminating) division in the group, which may well have actually weakened the leadership initiative and created factions that could impede the team in the long run.

Were the norms favoring decisiveness so strong that Chris could not speak up during the meeting and humbly challenge Pat's assertion? Might Pat have found a here-and-now Humble Inquiry way of involving Chris, the co-leader, before making a proclamation? The norms of the occupational (management) culture reflecting dominant assumptions of U.S. culture can become quite coercive in group meetings, which then tacitly reinforce the deeper assumption of competition between peers. Fortunately, in this case, Chris was willing to bring up the issue for review after the meeting and thus open the door to defining a different way forward for this group, if they really wanted shared leadership, group involvement, and collective decision-making. If Pat truly listened to Chris, they could work on how once again to become co-leaders and demonstrate real co-leadership to the group. Still, all too often the *damage done by the tell* changes the dynamic in the group in an undesirable way that may take some time to repair.

> **Competition and telling must be balanced with collaboration and Humble Inquiry.**

Why Is This Important Now?

There is, of course, much more to U.S. culture than what we've identified above. More important, things are continuing to change rapidly. We see culture evolving from where we have been in the eminently successful industrial machine age to a more technologically complicated, globally interconnected and fluid era. We have had to learn from terrorist attacks, severe pandemics, and climate change how to deal with VUCA (Volatility, Uncertainty, Complexity, and Ambiguity). The recognition of complex interdependencies is growing along with information technology, making the individualistic competitive biases in the culture more visible and potentially dysfunctional if not dangerous.

Consider, for example, the operating room of today, in which a surgeon, an anesthesiologist, key technicians, and nursing staff have to work in perfect harmony to succeed in a complex socio-technical operation. Consider that the many contributors to the procedure not only have different professions and ranks, but they are also equally likely to be of different generations and from different national macrocultures, which may have divergent values and norms around relationships and authority. For many such surgical team members, open and trusting Level 2 relationships are no longer optional but intrinsically necessary for successful task accomplishment.

Increasingly, tasks may resemble people on a seesaw.

Good performance in many team sports depends on *every* position doing its job or "the play" fails. A chorus has to practice *together* so that *every* member will be able to deal with all the musical variations that different conductors may demand. Flying a commercial airliner safely requires perfect coordination from the entire crew, as do all kinds of processes in the oil and gas, chemical, and nuclear industries. All of these group situations require the members of the group to build relationships with each other that go beyond just professionals working alongside each other. Checklists and other formal processes of coordination are not enough because they cannot flex sufficiently with unanticipated situations. Through Humble Inquiry, teams can build the Level 2 relationships that enable them to learn together. As they build higher levels of trust through joint learning, they become more open in their communication, which, in turn, enables them to deal with the inevitable surprises. Teamwork is not achieved by just getting the right people into the room, but by people *learning together* how to deal with interdependency.[5]

The irony is that when we see good task accomplishment resulting from Level 2 relationships and higher levels of trust, we admire it and almost treat it as a surprising anomaly. We know intuitively and from experience that we work better on a complex interdependent task with someone we know and trust, yet we are often not prepared to spend the effort, time, and money to ensure that such Level 2 relationships are built. We value such relationships when they are built as part of the work itself, as in military operations where soldiers form intense personal relationships with their brothers in arms. We admire their loyalty to each other and the heroism that is displayed on behalf of someone with whom one has a relationship. Yet when we see such deep relationships in business, we typically consider it note-worthy, sometimes even novel or innovative! Unfortunately, when budgets are getting crunched, no one is particularly surprised to see team-building programs (such as multi-day offsites) as some of the first cuts to be made.

In Conclusion

We see U.S. culture reinforcing tacit assumptions of prag-matism, individualism, competition, and status through achievement. These assumptions introduce a strong bias for getting the job done, which, combined with individual-ism, leads to a relative devaluing of relationship building, teamwork, and collaboration, except as means to the end of task accomplishment. Given those cultural biases, doing and telling are all too often valued more than asking, listening, and relationship building. However, as tasks become more complex and interdependent, collaboration, teamwork, and relationship building through Humble Inquiry may become critical for optimal task accomplishment—and survival.

READER EXERCISE

At a time when it isn't only futurists who see dramatic change as inevitable, we propose that the Humble Inquiry attitude will help us deal with this accelerating rate of change in our culture. The disruptions—if not upheavals—we face compel us to value inquiring more than telling. Do you agree that the Humble Inquiry mindset takes us from an old way—fitting what is going on into our existing models—to a new way of learning what is really going on?

Using the table that follows, reflect on the past chapter and your experience of culture and work. The table describes a relationship attitude and working mindset that evolves (a) From Telling to Inquiring, (b) From Transactional to Personal, (c) From Content to Context, and (d) From Interpreting and Influencing to Listening and Learning.

For each of the cells in this table, try jotting down some reflections on each of these mindsets. If you are moving from telling to inquiring, what is the telling mindset you are going to change, and what is the inquiring mindset you are going to adopt? Try doing this with each of the four transitions described. When you have completed this reflection, test it against "How we see it…" described on the following page.

From	To
Telling	Inquiring
Transactional	Personal
Content—What happened?	Context—What is really going on?
Interpreting and influencing	Listening and learning

(continued)

How we see it…

From	To
Telling: I have a role, a point of view and some data that I will apply to the question, dilemma, or problem at hand.	**Inquiring:** My role is less important than my team finding a more complete sense of what is really going on, so I will start by drawing other decision makers and their data into sense-making processes.
Transactional: We engage in an exchange of agreed-upon data to support our respective decision-making process. We maintain professional distance so that any emotional involvement will not interfere with our efficiently transacting our business.	**Personal:** We come together to tackle a complex problem that must be solved collectively. We engage in a purposeful learning process to build openness and trust in each other in order to share whatever information is relevant.
Content—What happened? Managers focus on the metrics that allow us to measure positive and negative outcomes, tightly defining desired states in measurable terms, looking for root causes when the metrics are off.	**Context—What is really going on?** Teams collect and assimilate metrics, probe for multiple causes and any related factors, assuming that they do not know what is really going on and that variance from metrics is not sufficient to explain the past or anticipate the future.
Interpreting and influencing: I have an intent and an agenda; I ask questions and interpret others' responses in this frame of reference so as to intervene to influence others' behavior in line with my intent.	**Listening and learning:** I have a purpose and accept that others are pursuing their purposes as well; we will share information in our mutual best interest if *we inquire further* in order to learn more and share more in return, in order to define our common purpose.

5

Cultural Do's and Don'ts of Conversation

In the previous chapter we discussed how the macrocultural forces of favoring task accomplishment over relationship building and telling over Humble Inquiry bias our interactions with each other and influence our patterns of behavior. Our interactions are driven in part by the cultural context operating in each specific situation. In other words, how we relate to another person, whether we tell or ask, whether we want to build more trust and openness, whether we just want acknowledgment or something more—these are best considered in terms of the cultural rules and norms that operate in a given *interpersonal situation*. That can be anything from a casual conversation with your boss to a formal meeting that you have organized or attend. In these kinds of situations we tend to ascribe actions to a person's personality or style. And yet, without thinking, most of us know what is situationally appropriate and behave accordingly. Generally, we have all learned the rules and the etiquette governing different situations, and that is precisely why culture is such a powerful force, particularly when the participants are of different rank or status.

The Cultural Proprieties of Status and Rank

In order to understand some of the inhibitors of Humble Inquiry, we should examine particularly the rules and norms pertaining to behavior between people of different statuses. From a subordinate's point of view, these rules can best be thought of as the *rules of deference*. In a typical hierarchy, how are subordinates supposed to show respect for their superiors? For example, when the superior is speaking, the subordinate is supposed to pay attention and not interrupt. It is noticeable and memorable if a team member of lower rank speaks up in a way that others would consider situationally inappropriate. Where tasks involve subcultures or the interaction of different macrocultures, misunderstanding of those rules can easily occur.

Turning our attention to the person in charge, he or she is supposed to command attention, maintain dignity, and project authority. We tend to have a very strong sense of discomfort when a leader of higher status says something that is obviously untrue or insulting, or does something that is immature and offensive. We enter situations with expectations about what is the appropriate demeanor for a high-status person, and it arouses anxiety and anger when those expectations are unfulfilled. There are stories of how twentieth-century executive headquarters had to provide private bathrooms for the CEOs so that they could properly compose themselves before appearing in public. In many organizations even today, the architecture of the building creates status distinctions by placing top managers in an executive suite that may only be accessible by private elevator or entrance. Yet even as these formal physical distinctions are eschewed in many contemporary organizations by putting senior executives in the very center of a floor of desks or cubicles, the organizational culture typically makes it clear through various informal scripts how those high-status persons are to be treated on a day-to-day basis and how they should appropriately display their status.

When we enter a new situation, meet someone and start a conversation, or go into a meeting, one of the first things that we sort out unconsciously is the relative status distinctions that may need to be observed. Some might argue we are still biologically programmed to locate ourselves in the pecking order. Humble Inquiry can be instrumental in such a situation because it provides an opportunity to find out whether the other person in the conversation is of higher or lower rank, whether you should be deferent or, alternatively, should expect deference. You can start by asking general questions: What kind of work do you do? What brings you here? Where did you work before you joined our firm?

This rank or status testing has become trickier but no less important in the contemporary workplace where antiquated *outward* signals of status such as uniforms are less and less relevant, less visible and, therefore, harder to decipher. We have all experienced, and celebrate, how it has become much harder to discern rank based on the visible artifacts, such as dress codes or name tags. Figuring out the situation based on who is in the choice/corner office locations does not work when there are no offices. Similarly, title and attire may mean little if rank and status are based upon the common knowledge that employees acquire as to who has the most technical prowess, number of granted patents, and so on. Understanding the real pecking order demands inquiry far beyond "Who do you work for?"

Some of what we observe today has resulted from efforts to "flatten the hierarchy" and loosen its attendant bureaucracy. And some will debate whether we may have gone too far. One of the few universals discovered by anthropologists is that *every* culture creates some form of hierarchy and status system, which is taught to young people and new-comers as a way to create sustainable order.

Because of the growing task interdependence between hierarchical tiers, a Humble Inquiry approach is useful here as well because in many of these situations the formal status will be far less relevant to improving the effectiveness of the team than figuring out who knows what regardless of status or rank. For the lower-status team members, establishing trust and openness may happen much faster with a little def-erence rather than scoring points or winning arguments. Similarly, the higher-status team members who are formally empowered to maximize the effectiveness of the team may find far more benefit in a Humble Inquiry approach that communicates "I know that we need each other to finish this task." It may be far more effective to acknowledge and reinforce an attitude of interdependence with open-ended questions that communicate to the lower-status team mem-bers that the higher-ups do not know all the answers, are not going to bark out orders, and will be mindful of the con-text of the situation and not just focus on the content of the task at hand.

Ultimately this may require that the higher-ups learn to ask for help from the lower-status contributors, all in the context of differing kinds of formal and informal role rela-tionships. Intentionally creating connections between rank levels through Humble Inquiry can play an important role, as the following example illustrates.

Getting Commitment across Organizational Tiers

When Ed was on the board of a regional environ-mental organization, the need for a new capital

campaign became evident. The CEO asked Ed to chair
a task force to investigate whether the board and the
organization were ready for the hard work of such
a campaign. A group of board members was then
selected by the CEO, and the first step was for Ed and
one other board member, with the CEO, to design
the opening meeting of this task force. Ed saw this as
an opportunity to build some deeper relationships
among the board members and therefore wanted
to begin with an informal dinner meeting. The CEO
thought this might be too expensive, but the other
board members volunteered to fund this dinner.

The CEO was particularly anxious to report at this
first meeting what mistakes had been made in a
previous capital campaign some years before. She
felt she had a great deal of knowledge that would
help this group to avoid some of the mistakes of the
past and clearly wanted to tell them what *she* thought
they needed to hear. Ed was uncomfortable with
this proposal because it put the challenge of the task
ahead of important relationship building, so he asked
her if after the informal dinner he could take over
the meeting to try a more dialogic approach. The
CEO grudgingly agreed, and Ed took the floor when
dessert had been served.

Ed: To get us started, I would like to propose that
while we have our dessert and coffee, why don't we go
around the room, in order starting at my left, speaking from the heart about why we belong here and why
each of us is committed to this organization. And it's
important that we not interrupt or comment until we

have all had a chance to speak from the heart. For myself, I would have to say that this has been some of the most meaningful work I've ever had a chance to do, and I have gotten to know a group of people who share this commitment and who are teaching each other how to be successful in this difficult work. I find that this organization is making a major contribution to our region and I love it.

In the following half-hour each person shared their feelings. The impact was almost magical: before that evening, most of those present knew each other only casually, but afterwards they saw each other as whole people who together discovered that they had the energy and passion to launch a difficult and critical capital campaign.

It also became clear to everyone that the way to involve the staff members of the organization was with this same dialogic process. Subsequent staff meetings featured brief recaps by the board members of those heartfelt reasons for belonging followed by each staff member sharing their reasons for committing to this organization. It was striking how much this process of revealing themselves to each other built commitment that then carried forth into the hard work of running the campaign for the next two years. Also surprising was how many staff members said that it was the first time they had heard this commitment from their board, which built confidence that the board and staff could work well together. The CEO was very happy with this new dialogic approach and realized there would be plenty of opportunities later on to *tell* the organization what mistakes to avoid.

Combining Task Performance
with Relationship Building

The above story not only deals with the question of status and authority but also leads directly to the central issue of being clear about *purpose*. Do we know why we are having a conversation or what our purpose is in calling a meeting? When you are meeting with a financial advisor or lawyer, visiting your doctor, or being introduced to your new head of marketing, do you ask yourself, What is the purpose of this meeting? Your purpose defines the task and the kind of relationships you want to create. When you come together with another person, you jointly and automatically define the situation: What is it we are here to do? What is each of our roles in the situation? What do we expect of each other? What kind of relationship can this be?

For our purposes, it is particularly useful to distinguish between task-oriented *transactional* relationships, in which one person needs something specific from the other person, and person-oriented *expressive* relationships. *Transactional relationships*, what we refer to as Level 1 relationships, tend to be clear and unambiguous. The relationship is a series of transactions for which a modicum of trust is beneficial to both parties. There is little sense of interdependence in that either person in either role could be replaced and the transaction would still occur. The tasks define the roles, and we pretty well know the rules of how to act.

Expressive relationships, akin to Level 2 and Level 3 relationships, are driven by personal needs to build the rela-tionship because one or both of the people involved become aware of their interdependence relative to a task and/or see personal emotional satisfaction in building a connection to the whole person. That is clearly what Ed had in mind when he launched the capital campaign task force. Knowing that the work of this group would require a lot of trust and commitment, he asked the board members to be expressive, to speak from the heart.

As we argued in the last chapter, the bias in U.S. culture in general, and business culture in particular, tends to be more transactional, to define most situations as "people getting together for the purpose of getting the job done, and perhaps little more than that." Again, this often leads to professional relationships that may involve an implicit effort by the relevant parties to actively avoid personal involvement with each other, even favoring professional distance as the best path to task accomplishment. Strictly task-oriented relationships may be designed to be impersonal and necessarily emotionally indifferent. Yet even though that definition of the situation seems culturally favored, as tasks become more complex and interdependent, you have to realize that as a manager/leader, *you have a choice*—rather than follow a cultural script, you can redefine the situation to be more relational, expressive, and personal.

Expressive personal relationships allow for, even expect, some emotional involvement intended to shrink professional distance. When we want to get to know someone better, we are moving into a Level 2 relationship, which should not be confused with the casual informality characteristic of many U.S. workplaces. If we want our direct reports to maintain the professional distance of a Level 1 relationship—because the task is well defined in terms of roles and handoffs—we can maintain that casual informality. However, it can be very confusing to the lower-ranking person because it implies a personal interest that may be just transactional and temporary. As teams become more multicultural, the risk of misreading informality as an encouragement to develop a more personal, Level 2 relationship increases greatly and requires efforts to explicitly examine how different cultures handle communication across status and hierarchical lines.

> **Increasing effectiveness may depend on building Level 2 relationships up, down, and across your organization**

Given growing task complexity and cultural diversity, the major organizational culture conundrum that emerges in our intricate globalized work context is whether it will be possible to maintain professionally distant status boundaries characteristic of traditional hierarchies, or whether more personal relationships become inevitable and desirable. Will certain industries continue to encourage and reinforce primarily transactional relationships in jobs that are governed by clear roles and rules? If so, will they be more vulnerable to automation and AI? It is hard to imagine such relationships being workable in situations where creativity and innovation require frequent open conversation, debate, and head-to-head negotiation. For now, it is most useful to think of a *continuum* that stretches from the extremely task oriented to the extremely personal and to ask how Humble Inquiry can help to draw people closer together *while maintaining situational propriety.*

Trust and Social Economics

To be humble, to ask instead of telling, or to *personize* the relationship to some degree requires a higher level of trust.[6] Yet *trust* is one of those words that we all think we know the meaning of only to discover that it is also highly situational. In the context of a personal conversation, trust is believing that the other person will acknowledge us and tell us the truth; we trust that other person will not take advantage of us, not embarrass or humiliate us, and, in the broader context, not cheat us. We expect the other person to work on our behalf, support the goals we have agreed to, and be willing to make and keep commitments.

All of this begins with *acknowledgment*. If you pass a stranger on the street and make eye contact, and then you both go on without further expression, that feels normal because you did not expect personal acknowledgment from a stranger. But if you see someone you know, you make eye contact, you smile, and yet the other person still shows no sign of recognition, then you may feel that something is amiss. You have not been recognized or acknowledged. It is this feeling of something being amiss that reminds us how much we count on mutual recognition and reciprocation. We may not remember someone's name, but our greeting and our demeanor tells the other person that we acknowledge them. Becoming socially invisible, ignored, or overlooked, can be traumatic.

We count on this trust as part of our social fabric. It is taken for granted that when we greet someone, whether it's a spoken hello or just a nod of the head, we expect a response of some kind. If we ask a question, we expect some kind of an answer. If we ask for help, we expect either to be helped or to be offered an explanation as to why we cannot be helped.

How can you convey to others that they can trust you? How do you show that you want to be helpful and caring without unwittingly offending people by offering something that they don't need or want? Generally, a key element is to learn to make yourself more vulnerable through Humble Inquiry. This can be challenging in that you risk being snubbed or ignored. If you let others in on your vulnerabilities, and they respond in a spirit of one-upmanship, assuming dominance or higher status because you were open with your Here-and-now Humility, how will you feel? Putting yourself out there and then being hung out to dry is personally and socially painful. To avoid this, we have many norms of etiquette about not embarrassing each other, to maintain "face" wherever possible, by which we mean that we should grant others their presented self, acknowledge them for who they want to be in a given situation, and expect them to acknowledge us in the same way. Revealing more about oneself than the situation might require is then an invitation to build the relationship to a higher level of trust and openness. The good news is that increasingly our culture rewards openness more than indifference, and entering expressive Level 2 relationships is far more satisfying than Level 1 transactionalism.

In Conclusion

The Humble Inquiry attitude is a powerful substrate for building relationships and making sense out of ambiguous situations. Humble Inquiry enables us to go beyond transactional civility in situations that involve personal and professional interdependencies across status boundaries. U.S. culture's emphasis on task performance, interpersonal competitiveness, and telling rather than asking, makes it more difficult to be humbly inquiring because we worry it may display weakness, real or perceived. Yet, paradoxically, only by learning to be more humbly inquiring and open to each other can we build up the mutual trust needed to work together most effectively.

Cultural rules define the basics and limits of conversations, but humans are multilayered systems who introduce their own biases and routines into the conversational process. In the chapters that follow we examine *intrapsychic* dynamics and show how Humble Inquiry is both inhibited and facilitated by our own cognitive and emotional biases.

READER EXERCISE

We have laid out what we see in U.S. culture and how we believe it shapes, coerces, encourages, and discourages both constructive and destructive interactions. Do you agree? Now is a good time to take stock and open up to your own "sense making." You may not really see it the way we do. Get it down on paper. Let it out. If there is something bugging you about what we've said so far, it's a great time for a journal-entry break. If you agree with what we have said, take a moment to think about a time when you experienced culture interfering with the conversational flow. Did cultural scripts of situational propriety prevent information from being shared? These are the cases we most need to learn from.

6

What Really Goes On in a Conversation

In order to fully understand the role of Humble Inquiry as a means of building a positive Level 2 relationship, we have to examine further the complexity of communication in the relationship-building process. We need to understand how cultural scripts—what is and is not appropriate to ask or to tell in a given situation—influence our *internal* communication process, that is, how we listen and how we choose to respond.

As we have pointed out, being a responsible member of society includes the acceptance of the rules of how to deal with each other and how to conduct conversations which show balance, equity, and mutual acceptance of each other's presented identities. When we are not acknowledged or feel that we are giving more than we are getting out of conversations, or when we feel talked down to, we may feel agitated, disrespected, offended, even humiliated. Humble Inquiry should be a reliable way to avoid these negative reactions in a conversation. So why don't we respond with Humble Inquiry more routinely and why is this potentially difficult?

One reason may be that we are not seeking to build a positive relationship—we may want to be one up and win. We may even be tempted to use Humble Inquiry as a ploy to draw the other person out in order to gain advantage.

As we will see, it is a dangerous ploy because we are inevitably sending mixed signals, and our lack of sincerity may do more harm than good. In that instance, we can actually weaken the relationship and create distrust.

A second reason is that there are, in all cultures, specific rules about what it is *not okay* to ask or talk about in certain situations. We need to proceed with caution as we try to *personize* relationships through Humble Inquiry. Such caution is particularly important when we are conversing with people from other cultures, such as when we are trying to decipher what is appropriate openness with respect to authority and trust building. In this chapter we present an *interpersonal* model that explores this issue and explains why we may send mixed signals, why insincere Humble Inquiry can make matters worse, why interpersonal feedback is so complicated, and how the Humble Inquiry attitude can help us avoid some of these difficulties.

The Johari Window: Four Parts of Our Socio-Psychological Self

The Johari window is a useful simplification first invented by Joe Luft and Harry Ingham to explain the complexity of communication.[7] In Diagram 6.1, Person A and Person B are in a conversational "seesaw" with each other.

THE OPEN SELF AND NORMAL COMMUNICATION (ARROW 1)

We each enter every situation or budding relationship with a culturally informed *open self* that will reflect our purpose for being there. We present ourselves to each other by our physical stance, tone of voice, and, most important, the topics that we bring up. With a stranger in a new situation, it

Diagram 6.1 The Back and Forth of Conversation

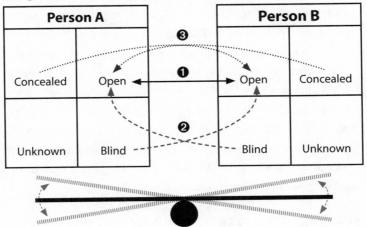

may be the weather, where you are from, or task-related information. We have all learned what is appropriate in different transactional situations. What we talk about with a sales associate and what we talk about with a stranger at a party are different, but both are quite circumscribed by the surrounding culture. We are taught what is potentially too personal and should be avoided in such conversations. Only if we have already built a Level 2 relationship would this more personal communication be appropriate.

THE BLIND SELF AND UNWITTING COMMUNICATION (ARROW 2)

As we converse with others, we send a variety of signals above and beyond the intentional signals sent from our open self. Our body language, tone of voice, timing and cadence of speech, clothing and accoutrements, and what we do with our eyes all convey something to the other person, who forms a total impression of us based on all of the signals sent. Some of this information is culturally scripted, such as good eye contact means one is paying attention. However, much of this information is ambiguous and passed on without our being aware of it. This means we need to realize that in every conversation we also have a *blind self*, the signals we are sending *without being aware* that we are sending them, which nevertheless create the impression that others have of us. This level of communication raises the issue of authenticity or sincerity inasmuch as we may unwittingly be sending mixed or even contradictory messages simultaneously. It is our realization that we all have a blind self that often motivates us to get feedback from others.

THE CONCEALED SELF—COMMUNICATION DILEMMAS AND CHOICES (ARROW 3)

Our *concealed self* is all the things we know about ourselves and others but are not willing or supposed to reveal because it might offend or hurt others or might be too embarrassing to ourselves. As we grow up, we are trained in our cultural values and norms to know what is acceptable and what is not. For example, we have learned that it is *not* acceptable to reveal a great deal of what we perceive and feel about the other person in the exchange or transaction.

We have also learned that in order to protect our sense of self-esteem, we must conceal from others negative things about ourselves: insecurities that we are ashamed to admit, feelings and impulses that we consider negative or inconsistent with our self-image, or moments from the past when we failed or performed badly. And, most important, we hide our reactions to other people that would be impolite or hurtful to reveal to them.

Of course the other persons in the conversation are also bound by cultural rules to conceal their impressions of us and their reactions to our blind selves, which produces one of the great ironies of social life: the impressions offered by our blind selves can be the subject of gossip but may never be revealed to us, hence the label *blind*. We know that we form impressions of others, so we must be aware that others form impressions of us. Unless we create special circumstances that bend the rules of culture, we may go through an entire lifetime without ever finding out what some others really think about us.

Society ultimately relies on our acknowledging and accepting each other as much as possible in terms of how we present ourselves. The flaws, anomalies, weaknesses, and failures we see in others are by design not normally revealed because negative, unsolicited reactions not only impact the others' positive image of self but also stimulate retaliation, which could threaten our own self-esteem. Only as we develop closer relationships with others do we find it easier to share some of our reactions. In fact, one of the ways we judge the openness of a relationship is the degree to which we reveal our concealed feelings about ourselves and each other. At the same time, some of what we learn removes some of our blind spots and increases the likelihood that we will come across as authentic and sincere.

THE UNKNOWN SELF

The fourth self—the *unknown self*—refers to those things that neither I nor the people with whom I have relationships know about me. I may have hidden talents that come out in a brand new situation, I may have all kinds of unconscious thoughts and feelings that surface from time to time, and I may have unpredictable responses based on psychological or physical factors that catch me by surprise. I have to be prepared for the occasional unanticipated feelings or behaviors that pop out of me.

Authenticity and Sincerity

In judging others, we frequently refer to some people as coming across as sincere or authentic. We consider these important attributes, especially in our bosses and leaders. How do we make that judgment? Over time, we base our degree of trust on how consistent their behavior is, how much they do what they say, and how much they honor their commitments. The Johari window model points to an important additional source of information that we get in the here-and-now conversation: how *consistent* the signals are that come from the open self and the blind self. We know from psychological studies that some of what we think, feel, and want to do are sufficiently culturally unacceptable that we suppress and even *repress* those thoughts, feelings, and impulses.

Generally, these insights from the unknown self come to our consciousness only when counseling or external events bring them up to our concealed self. At the same time, to our surprise and chagrin, we sometimes discover in a deeper conversation that some of what we conceal from ourselves—our unknown selves—is quite visible to others and therefore becomes part of our blind selves. Sometimes we display to others through our blind selves the very same insecurities and inappropriate impulses and feelings that we are trying to conceal *even from ourselves,* thereby creating the impression that we are insincere or not authentic. Others often notice our symptoms of tension or insecurity, such as a trembling hand or a sweaty brow, even before we do. Yet if one were to ask us if we're feeling nervous, we might deny it, brush it off, especially in Level 1 interactions.

When relationships go wrong, one of the most common reasons is that person A, as depicted in Diagram 6.1, believes he or she is communicating clearly while person B experiences mixed or conflicting signals and therefore decides to withdraw from further involvement, reflecting a sense of growing mistrust.

Getting to Know Each Other

A useful way to build a relationship is for people to open up more of their concealed selves, especially their reactions to each other and what signals they receive from the other's blind self. This has the effect of reducing the relative size of the blind self. We realize that in a relationship-building process the most difficult issue is how far to go in revealing something that normally we would conceal, knowing at the same time, that unless we open up more, we will have a harder time building the relationship. When such opening up is planned and formatted, as in special workshops or meetings designed for the purpose of improving relationships, we label this category of communication *feedback* and value it because it removes some of our blind spots. Such feedback can work precisely because the workshop intentionally legitimizes suspending the cultural rules that would normally make it unacceptable because *unsolicited* feedback is generally a countercultural process.

The contortions we go through to get *honest* feedback mirror the cultural restrictions we place on not telling each other face to face what we really think of each other. The reluctance we display when someone asks us for feedback mirrors the degree to which we are afraid to offend or humiliate. We duck the issue by trying to emphasize positive feedback, knowing full well that what the others may really want to hear is where we see them as wanting or imperfect, so that they can improve. We see all our own imperfections because the concealed self is filled with self-doubt and self-criticism, and we wonder whether others perceive the same flaws. And, of course, they probably do, but they would not want to tell us, in part because that would license us to tell them about their flaws, and we could then both lose in a self-esteem race to the bottom. Remember that it is the very essence of civilized society to maintain a modicum of each others' self-esteem as much as possible, most of the time.

Gently asking about and/or revealing something that is culturally defined as *personal* are ways we break out of this normative dilemma. The essence of the Humble Inquiry attitude is to drop the professional, task-oriented, transactional self and either ask about or reveal something that clearly has nothing to do with the purpose of the transaction, which invites acknowledgment and a more personal response. The Humble Inquiry attitude can, in that sense, be expressed *not* with a question but by revealing something personal about oneself as a prelude to humbly inquiring about the other person. We can choose to tell something to the other that reveals Here-and-now Humility in order to open the door to *personizing* the conversation.

If these early revelations and questions are acknowledged and reciprocated, the relationship can develop and allow for going deeper. This mutual exploration process has to be slow and carefully calibrated because the cultural forces for situational propriety are very coercive. In a relationship across hierarchical boundaries it may be necessary for the higher-status person to start this process not with a bunch of personal questions to her team but with a revelation about herself. If managers and leaders really want to know what their groups think about them, it may help to start with revealing some of their own personal goals and ask their group for feedback on how they, the managers, are doing in relation to those goals. In general, a great deal can be exchanged before the relationship gets to the personal feedback stage, and even then, it probably works best if it stays on matters that both parties have agreed to, such as their shared goals and objectives. All of these choices and contingencies remind us that interpersonal communication and relationship building are always complex interactive dances.

> **The goal of relationship building should be to reduce each other's blind spots by each revealing more of our concealed selves.**

The Dance of Conversation

Try visualizing the conversation between two people getting to know each other as a dance in which "who leads" becomes irrelevant as the conversation evolves. Where and how does the Humble Inquiry attitude come into play through asking, listening to each other, revealing, and responding? How each of these components plays a critical role in relationship building is illustrated in the following example: Leading a product group, Morgan meets a new group member and is committed to getting to know the person better, above and beyond the immediate job description. Morgan takes a Humble Inquiry approach.

Morgan and Taylor Get to Know Each Other

Morgan: Tell me a bit about yourself…

Taylor reflects on Morgan's inquiry and decides to adopt a positive attitude by assuming that Morgan's Humble Inquiry is an intentional move toward building a personal relationship and decides to open up a bit.

Taylor: Well, for one thing I am very happy to be joining this group because I had always hoped I might be asked to join you. I have admired the work of this group and hope I can contribute.

Morgan listens very carefully for the here-and-now message, calibrating the sincerity of Taylor's words. Deciding that they sound genuine, Morgan builds the relationship by revealing and then following up with more Humble Inquiry.

Morgan: I am glad to hear that, because I really wanted you on this team. Tell me a little more about your experience here.

Now Taylor listens very carefully to decide whether Morgan is sincere with this question, relying on personal experiences to aid in that assessment. Satisfied, Taylor decides to reveal more.

Taylor: Well, I started in the production department, but I never really got along with the head of that group. I wanted a more collaborative atmosphere and heard good things about your group, so I applied to transfer to here.

Still listening carefully, Morgan is intrigued by Taylor's reference to a *collaborative atmosphere* because Morgan has been working hard at building collaboration to deal with the high interdependencies that their work involves. Morgan decides to reinforce this shared value of collaboration, to explore some of Taylor's perceptions, and maybe even get some feedback from a new voice.

Morgan: I am very glad that you are approaching our work as collaborative because our success is very dependent upon all of you helping each other and helping me. By the way, I am curious how you and others perceive this group?

Taylor listens carefully to get a feel for whether it is safe to tell Morgan what some others have said about this product group, knowing that Morgan may not have heard this from other people. Providing this feedback would reveal part of Taylor's concealed self, which is risky.

Taylor: I can see how important collaboration is to solve the complex problems this group faces. I will say that I have heard from others that they saw this group as having wishy-washy leadership, and did not see how one could get ahead in your group. In fact, I wanted to be here because I wanted to learn how to work collaboratively in this group, regardless of that feedback.

Morgan listens, fighting off inner messages of dismay and defensiveness, ("wishy washy"?!) and decides to accept the feedback and, at the same time, reassure Taylor that it was okay to reveal these perceptions. Morgan believes that they are building a good positive relationship and decides to lay out the group's managerial philosophy immediately, including a concrete next step to reinforce this philosophy.

Morgan: I'm so glad you felt safe enough to tell me what some others thought even though it was— ouch!—a little negative. I also find it reassuring that what they see is what I am actually trying to do. I want to build the norm in this group that unless we collaborate, we won't get the job done. I know, as your manager, that I don't have all the answers and I depend on you to step in and provide some leadership. In this group we try to recognize how important it is to be open with each other so that we can trust each other rather than compete for glory points or personal advancement. As a manager I pay particular attention to behavior that is helpful and collaborative and open. You are taking on a job where several people report to you. I believe that the most important thing for you to do is to build a personal relationship with each of them. Let's meet for breakfast next week and discuss how things are going.

Taylor feels reassured that the reporting relationship with the new manager apparently won't stifle communication. That said, Taylor is also a little uncertain, based on prior experience in more competitive groups, how this will actually work out. It's clear that Morgan will evaluate how Taylor handles direct reports and builds trusting collaborative relationships with them. For this reason, Taylor especially appreciates that the door has been opened, that the next step in the relationship has been identified, and wants to show appreciation.

Taylor: I understand what you're saying. I look forward to observing how you and the group build these collaborative norms, and I look forward to sharing what I've learned at our breakfast meeting next week.

Both Morgan and Taylor part with a feeling of having opened some relational doors, even though they have not talked about Taylor's specific job role other than the imperative of building a mutual understanding of the norms of openness and collaboration.

Humble Inquiry functions as an invitation to be more personal and is therefore the key to building a Level 2 relationship. Both parties need to engage in this process. If Taylor wanted to open the door to a more personal relationship (revealing the concealed self), but Morgan didn't, we could expect the conversation to become awkward quickly since Taylor reports to Morgan. How we listen and how we respond is equally determined by each person's attitude. The dance does not work unless both parties decide to cooperate and build a relationship of openness and trust.

Conversations are inevitably complicated because the messages are layered and nuanced even if the sender intends them to be very simple and direct. It is important to become aware of the different parts of yourself, how each of your perceptions of the other's blind self creates impressions of sincerity or insincerity, and how the blind self can be made more visible only if you each decide to reveal part of your concealed self. Through the interaction and feedback, both Morgan and Taylor expanded their open selves by revealing more of their concealed selves, and therefore became more aware of their blind selves.

In Conclusion

Humble Inquiry aids your *personizing* process by projecting your attitude of interest and curiosity, asking questions to which you do not know the answers. The implementation can be complex because either you are not sure what you should be curious about, or your questions can be misunderstood or even culturally inappropriate. Being curious about and asking about something can easily become too personal and lead the other person to be put off. Therefore, relationship building through the seesaw of asking and revealing always has to occur within the situational norms of what is and is not appropriate, unless or until both parties develop enough trust to agree to expand those boundaries as they each take some risks in getting to know each other better.

READER EXERCISE

Take a recent conversation that you have had and try to diagram it with your own comments of what was going on, the way we did with Morgan and Taylor. Identify, as well, the things that could have been said to make the conversation better, in the sense of aligning it to your purpose or meeting your goals.

7

What Goes On inside Your Head?

Our "performances" in conversations are deeply dependent on what is going on inside our heads. We cannot be appropriately humble if we misread or misinterpret the situation we are in and either ignore or do not know what is appropriate in that situation. We need to see how our minds constantly create biases, perceptual distortions, and inappropriate impulses. To be effective in Humble Inquiry, we must make an effort to learn what these biases and distortions are and figure out how to avoid them when they interfere with relationship building, helping, and sense making.

To begin this learning, consider this simple model of processes that are, in fact, extremely complicated. Our nervous system simultaneously gathers data, processes data, proactively manages what data to gather, and decides how to react. What we see and hear and how we react to things are partly driven by our needs, purposes, and expectations. Though these processes occur more or less simultaneously, it is useful to distinguish them and treat them as a cycle.

Diagram 7.1 shows how, in a split second, we *observe* (O), *react* (R), make *judgments* (J), and then *intervene* (I).

In the relational context we use the term *intervene* rather than *act* because even doing nothing, remaining si-

Diagram 7.1 The ORJI Cycle

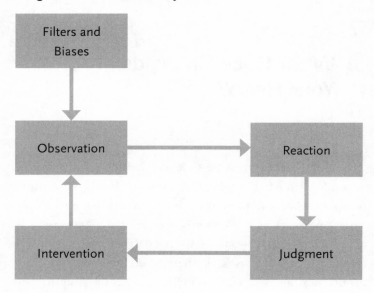

lent, looking away, or losing eye contact are interventions
with consequences for the interaction. In other words, it is
very important to know that *everything you do* in an interaction is an *intervention that will have some kind of impact on
others.* The other person will immediately launch his or her
own ORJI cycle no matter how much or how little we do.
Knowing that all your actions are really interventions with
various kinds of outcomes, it is important to figure out when
things go wrong, when you are misunderstood or have offended someone, where in the cycle things got off track. Was
your observation inaccurate, did you have an inappropriate
emotional response, or did you make a bad judgment as the
basis of your intervention? Learning to analyze your own
behavior will help you to intervene more effectively and get
the results in the relationship that you intended.

Observation

Observation should be the accurate registering, through all of our senses, of what is actually occurring in the environment and what the demands are of the situation in which we find ourselves. In reality, the nervous system is both a passive register and a proactive data seeker, programmed through many prior experiences to seek and filter incoming information. We distort to an unknown degree what we perceive. We block out a great deal of information that is potentially available if it does not fit our preconceptions, expectations, needs, and purpose.

We do not passively register information; we do not passively observe. We actively, even if subconsciously, select out from the available data what we are capable of registering and classifying, based on our language and learned concepts (culture) as well as what we want and need. To put it more dramatically, we do not think and talk about what we see; we see what we are *able* to think and talk about. Hence, the ORJI cycle effectively starts from our filters and biases.

Psychoanalytic and cognitive theories have shown how significant perceptual distortions can be. Perhaps the clearest examples are the defense mechanisms *denial* and *projection. Denial* is refusing to see certain categories of information as they apply to us, and *projection* is seeing in others what is actually operating in us and shows up in our blind self. It has also been shown that our needs distort our perceptions, such as when our thirst makes us perceive that every mirage in the desert is an oasis. To deal with reality, to strive for objectivity, to attempt to see how things really are, as artists attempt to do when they want to draw or paint realistically, we must understand and attempt to reduce the initial distortions that our perceptual system creates.

Reaction

The ORJI cycle diagram shows emotional reactions occurring as a result of what we observe, but there is growing evidence that the emotional response may actually occur simultaneously with, if not prior to, the observation. Humans can experience fear physically before they identify the actual threat. This being the case, the most difficult aspect of learning about our emotional reactions is that we often do not notice them at all. We deny feelings or take them so much for granted that we, in effect, short-circuit them and move straight into judgments and actions (interventions). We may be feeling anxious, angry, guilty, embarrassed, aggressive, or joyful, yet we may not realize that we are feeling something, and even then, may not be sure what we are feeling.

A common example occurs when we are driving and someone unexpectedly cuts in front of us, and triggers a reaction. The momentary feeling of *threat* triggers the observation that the person is cutting us off, and we *react* with negative intent stemming from the instantaneous *judgment* that the other driver has no right to do that, and then to the *intervention* that we swerve away, or pull up alongside the "offender" to shout or gesticulate. The reaction results in a premature judgment and action that may mislead us from the safer alternative of slowing down to allow the other car to do its thing while we live to drive another day.

Feelings are very much a part of every moment of living, but we learn early in life that there are many situations where feelings should be controlled, suppressed, overcome, and in various other ways denied. As we learn gender roles and occupational roles, and as we become socialized into a particular culture, we learn which feelings are acceptable and which ones are not, when it is appropriate to express feelings and when it is not, when feelings are "good" and when they are "bad."

In our pragmatic task-oriented culture we also learn that feelings are a source of distortion and should not influence judgments, and we are often cautioned not to act impulsively on our feelings. But, paradoxically, we may end up acting *most* on our feelings when we are *least* aware of them, all the while deluding ourselves that we are carefully acting only on rational assessments. We are often surprisingly oblivious to the influences that our feelings have on our judgments.

It is not impulsiveness per se that causes difficulty. It is acting on impulses that are not consciously understood, and hence not evaluated prior to the action, that can get us into trouble. The major issue around feelings, then, is to find ways of getting in touch with them so that we can increase our span of reactions. It is essential for us to be able to know what we are feeling, both to avoid bias in reacting and to use those feelings as a diagnostic indicator of what may be happening, particularly in the relationships we are trying to develop.

Practicing Humble Inquiry before we react becomes an important way of preventing unfortunate consequences. Recall the story of the graduate student who shouted at his daughter for interrupting his studying instead of asking her why she had knocked on the door. He was angry at the interruption and let his anger determine his reaction without checking whether it was appropriate at that moment. An important use of Humble Inquiry in this regard is to inquire of oneself before one acts. Can you take a moment to ask yourself, How am I reacting? before you go to judgment and action. If the driver had asked that question before speeding up, he or she might have recognized the sense of threat and followed up with this question: Why would I become angry and risk an accident when I don't even know why this other driver cut in front of me? If the other car was heading to the hospital because its passenger was about to deliver a baby, it would be a mistake to slow them down.

Judgment

We are constantly processing data, analyzing information, evaluating, and making judgments. This ability to analyze prior to action is what makes humans capable of planning sophisticated behaviors to achieve complex goals and to sustain a series of steps that take us years into the future. The capacity to plan ahead and to organize our actions according to plan is a unique aspect of human intelligence.

Being able to reason *logically* is, of course, essential. But all of the analyses and judgments we engage in are worth only as much as the data on which they are based. It does little good to go through sophisticated planning and analysis exercises if we do not pay attention to the manner in which the information we use is acquired and how biases may have already distorted such information. Nor does analysis help us if we let our emotional reactions bias our reasoning. It has been shown that even under the best of conditions we are capable of only limited rationality and make systematic cognitive errors.[8] We should at least try to minimize the distortions in the initial information intake process, and with eyes wide open, remember that Humble Inquiry is one reliable way of gathering data which requires that we implicitly restrain the tendency to *judge* as we *ask*.

Intervention

Once we have made some kind of judgment, we act, even if this looks like no overt action at all. The judgment may be no more than the decision to respond to an emotional impulse, but it is a judgment nevertheless, and it is important to be aware of it. In other words, when we act impulsively, it seems as if we are short-circuiting the rational judgment process. In fact, what we are doing is not short-circuiting—it is giving too much credence to an initial observation and our emotional response to it. Knee-jerk reactions that get us into trouble are interventions that are judgments based on incorrect or incomplete data, or they may be just emotional impulses. If someone is attacking me and I react with an instant counterattack, that may be a valid and appropriate intervention. But if I have misperceived, and the person was not attacking me at all, then my counterattack makes me look like the aggressor and may lead to a serious communication breakdown, or worse, a physical altercation.

> **Disciplined, careful observation and genuine curiosity minimize the likelihood of bad judgment and inappropriate behavior.**

In the culture of do and tell, the biggest problem is that we cannot really know how valid or appropriate what we tell or are told is to the situation, *unless we ask*. If we want to build a relationship with someone to open up communication channels, we have to keep our eyes wide open to avoid operating on incorrect or unvalidated data as much as we can. Being curious and checking things out by asking in a humble manner then becomes a core activity of relationship building and collective sense making.

Reconstruction of the ORJI cycle, in reflection afterwards, often reveals that one's judgment is logical but is based on what are perceived to be facts yet which may be neither accurate nor complete. Hence the outcome may not be logical at all. It follows, therefore, that the most dangerous part of the cycle is the first step, where we take it for granted that what we perceive is valid enough to act on. We make attributions and prejudgments rather than focusing as much as possible on what really happened and what the other person really meant. The time when Humble Inquiry is often most needed is when we observe something that makes us angry or anxious. It is at those times that we need to slow down, to ask ourselves and others "What's really going on?" in order to check out the facts. Then we ask ourselves how valid our reactions are before we make a judgment and leap into action.

Let's use the ORJI cycle to analyze the graduate student who yelled at his daughter when she knocked on the door. He *observed* her arrival, *reacted* with anger to it, *judged* it to be inappropriate and, therefore, *intervened* by yelling at her. Now imagine the conversation the next morning when the graduate student's wife told him that he had been rude and punishing when she had simply encouraged the daughter to go down and say goodnight and offer a cup of coffee:

Confronting a Misunderstanding

Wife: Why on earth did you yell at her? (Confrontive inquiry)

Husband: I had explicitly told her at dinner not to disturb me. (A tell)

Wife: But she said you never gave her a chance to explain why she was there. She told me that all she said was "Hi, Daddy," and you yelled at her. (New data for sense making)

Husband: She interrupted my train of thought. That made me angry (reaction) and I was reminded that she often disobeys. (Judgment, and possibly an unconscious bias of judging the daughter as disobedient and needing to be taught a lesson, in the form of a tell)

Wife: So, was anger appropriate *at that moment* when she just said "Hi, Daddy" in a friendly way after knocking on the door? (Diagnostic inquiry)

Husband: Well, she caught me at a bad moment when I was just trying to finish a thought. (A self-justifying tell to add to sense making)

Wife: Well that doesn't sound fair. Your anger was based on your own feelings—not on what she did. (Questioning the logic in an effort to make sense)

Husband: But I had told her not to interrupt. (A defensive tell)

Wife: So, she was wrong, no matter what? What if she had come down to tell you the house was on fire—would you have yelled at her then? (Confrontive inquiry)

Husband: Of course not, but how was I supposed to know that you sent her down? I was busy and preoccupied. (The key question the husband needs to think about: why not check before acting?)

Wife: So you upset both your daughter and me with a knee-jerk reaction based on your feelings of the moment, did not take a moment to ask what was going on, and let your immediate feeling lead to a wrong judgment and inappropriate action. (The wife confronts with a strong tell. She might also consider what she can learn from having decided to send the daughter instead of going down herself.)

Husband: I am sorry, but I am also wondering why you sent her down instead of coming yourself. You knew I was tense. (The husband sees his error and now confronts his wife to examine her own ORJI cycle and why she did what she did.)

What are the *critical questions* when things go wrong? What did each of them do that created the unpleasant situation? What could either of them have done differently? It seems the answer almost always is to check your observation. Ask yourself whether what you are feeling and judging is based on accurate here-and-now data or is based on what you expected, feared, hoped for, and in other ways preprogrammed yourself to observe.

We register a great deal but also filter via our unconscious biases and our current intentions. We see and hear more or less what we expect or anticipate based on prior experience, or, more importantly, on what we hope to achieve—our wants, needs, and purposes—in addition to the immediate context in which we are operating. Conversations always occur in a context, and the need to tell or "fix" often arises out of that context rather than from personality or broad social forces. When things go awry and cause hurt or negative feelings, re-examining the process with an attitude of Here-and-now Humility or curiosity can bring the relationship back into harmony and starkly reveal the consequences of not asking in a Humble Inquiry way in the first place.

In Conclusion

When we consider the two communication models together (the seesaw or dance of conversation in Chapter 6, and the ORJI cycle here), we can see that even ordinary conversation is a complicated exchange involving moment-to-moment decisions on what to say, how to say it, and how to respond to what others say. What we choose to reveal is very much a product of our perception of the situation and our understanding of the cultural scripts that apply in that situation. Our initial biases in what we perceive and feel, how we judge situations, and how we react all reflect our culture, our personal history, and our immediate context. Our perceptions of our roles, ranks, and statuses within a given situation predispose us to assume that we know what is appropriate. Situations in which participants have different perceptions of their roles, ranks, and statuses are, therefore, the most vulnerable to miscommunication and unwitting offense or embarrassment. It is, in fact, a miracle that we communicate as well as we do, especially when rigid hierarchy is there to create "order" (by reinforcing preconceptions!).

Intrinsic to the Humble Inquiry attitude is a commitment to becoming more mindful of how we operate, and possibly needing to unlearn some of the scripted behavior that results from our inculcation. Our genetically coded temperament, our learned personality, and, above all, our socialization into situationally appropriate behavior operate all the time and often get us into trouble or prevent us from communicating openly and completely. The attitude of Humble Inquiry is, in the end, both a positive way to build better relationships and an analytical way to begin the learning process toward this goal. An unshakeable conclusion that keeps emerging is that the safest and often the most effective intervention when tension arises in a conversation is some form of Humble Inquiry.

READER EXERCISE

The last two chapters are full of models and theory, not to mention plenty of our opinions. The best way to find your own opinion on this is to go through the deconstruction, or unpacking, process. Think about a conversation that really worked, one in which you and others really made progress. Did you find the progress in revelations of concealed or blind selves? Did it happen by drawing out deep beliefs or deeper insecurities that freed up logjams? You can also try thinking about conversations that left you feeling "meh" or ones that did did not go well. Did you go in with an assessment of the situation that was not accurate, where you thought you knew what was going on and how to make progress, only to discover you had it all wrong? Can you break the situation down using the ORJI cycle model to sort out what went wrong and what was *really* going on?

8
Developing the Attitude of Humble Inquiry

The skills of asking in general and Humble Inquiry in particular help in three broad domains: (1) in your personal life with your loved ones and in all aspects of your social life; (2) in your organizations, to identify needs for collaboration among interdependent work units and to facilitate such collaboration; and (3) in your role as leader or manager, to create the relationships and the climate that will promote the open communication and trust needed for effective and safe task performance.

The attitudes and behaviors required in each of these three areas are to some degree countercultural and may, therefore, require some *unlearning* and *new learning*. In particular, some broadening of perspective and insight may be needed to help you identify when and where you could do less telling and more asking.

> We will all need to think broadly and deeply about the role of relationships in the VUCA world of the future and discover the benefits of more Humble Inquiry in making sense of what is actually going on.

The Two Anxieties of Unlearning and New Learning

Learning new things can be easy when there is no unlearning involved. But if the new learning has to displace some old
habits of telling, two anxieties come into play that have to be
managed. First, *survival anxiety* is the realization that unless we learn the new behavior, we will be at a disadvantage
(metaphorically threatened by extinction). Survival anxiety
provides the motivation to learn, even if it is mostly nervous
energy.

As we confront the learning task and develop new attitudes and behaviors, we often realize it may be difficult,
or we may not want to tolerate the period of incompetence
or uncertainty while we learn. Similarly, we realize that our
colleagues or friends may not understand or welcome our
new behavior. And, worst of all, we might not like the new
identity that the new learning would require us to adopt.
The "I got this" rugged individualist just may not want to become a humble inquirer.

When we anticipate all of these potential difficulties,
we are experiencing *learning anxiety,* which often accompa-
nies any unlearning and is the primary source of resistance
to change. As long as learning anxiety remains stronger than
survival anxiety, we will resist change and avoid learning.

One might argue then that in order to learn, one must
increase survival anxiety, yet this only increases our overall
tension because the sources of learning anxiety do not go
away. To facilitate new learning, we need to *decrease learning anxiety.* We need to feel that a new behavior or practice
is worthwhile, not threatening, and possible to learn. And
we need to know that there will be guidance, coaching, and
support to get us started. We also need to be confident that
there will be opportunities to practice throughout the process. If what we are learning is somewhat countercultural,

we need to be provided a safe situation in which we can practice. If we fear our group's disapproval, the new learning often works best if the group takes up the learning challenge together. If we fear the loss of our current identity, we need to find some positive reasons for adopting a new way of doing things.

We have attempted through theory and stories to provide some positive reasons for adopting a Humble Inquiry attitude. It remains up to the reader to judge what resonates and what helps. For now, we've created some guidelines to get you started.

Some Ideas to Help You Unlearn and Learn

SLOW DOWN AND VARY THE PACE

Think about our relay race metaphor, where runners learn to accelerate to top speed and rapidly decelerate to handoff speed. Changing pace, taking stock, observing ourselves and others, and adapting our behavior may not come as naturally in the work ethos of individualism and competition that we described in Chapter 4. Slowing down is countercultural for many, and varying the pace to coordinate with others may seem a bit inefficient. This is a time to think about survival anxiety and experiment by testing learning anxiety. Is it possible to find a shared work *pace* that allows for the group to accomplish more? Is it worth it to take a time-out on a project to reflect on what worked and what did not? What may seem to be less efficient may turn out to be more effective.

DON'T GIVE IN TO THE PERILOUS PRESSURE OF "FAST IS BETTER"

We spend a lot of effort finding ways to increase our pace of response; this is another not-so-subtle subtext in American business and social culture. In some categories of new product/system development and production, we accelerate to produce version 1.0 knowing that it is even faster to produce version 1.1 if we have discovered faults or errors in our first design. This "fail fast" mindset may work for software and many consumer goods that can be reworked or reprinted so quickly that there is more to be gained by redoing quickly rather than slowing down to get it done better in the first place.

All of this may work very well when failing fast negatively impacts only machines, microprocessors, manufacturing robots, 3D printers, algorithms, and AI. These intelligent assistants to human processes may have some "memory," but they do not (for now) have feelings. The problem with humans in groups is that we have strong feelings about ourselves and about the other people with whom we have relationships. While "fail fast" fits very well into the culture of do and tell, it may not fit as well with our human intent to inquire and reflect. The bot that you reprogram does not care and is not offended. But when you impulsively react to a human colleague—whether you are telling, rebuking, praising, or ignoring—that colleague probably *does* care, might even be offended, and thereafter may not share the truth of what is actually going on. Rebuilding human relationships is a slower process than fixing or adapting an algorithm or prototype. Humble Inquiry is in the end an *attitude* to first ask and reflect. To speed up this process risks failing fast with human relationships that cannot as easily be reprogrammed in the next iteration.

Hurrying also has this insidious way of blinding us from seeing the broader context, by obscuring new possibilities, discouraging us from considering other options.

By contrast, learning Humble Inquiry is not learning how to run faster but how to slow down just enough to observe carefully and take full stock of situational reality so as to ensure that the baton is not dropped.

SET UP LEARNING TIME WITH OTHERS AND SLOW DOWN TOGETHER

If successful task accomplishment requires building a new relationship with a colleague on whom you will be dependent, this process need not take very long. *Personizing* the relationship—doing something informal together, such as meeting away from work for a walk or a meal—need not be a big production. But it may take a different pace. Any manager or leader can do that and should be open to requests from other members of the organization to engage in this way. Obviously there are very real limits to how much senior leadership can engage personally with many members of a large organization. The new perspective, however, is to be open, flexible, and welcoming of this kind of engagement, at least with your direct reports or closest collaborators. It may sound inefficient to invest in this unstructured relationship building up front, rather than immediately getting down to work on the task at hand. Yet taking time to focus on relationship building at the beginning may very quickly establish openness and trust. This leap of faith will later allow for greater collective acceleration toward *more effective* task accomplishment.

REFLECT BY *ASKING YOURSELF* HUMBLE INQUIRY QUESTIONS

It is hard to know when it is appropriate to inquire and when to tell unless we get better at assessing the nature of the situation we are in, what the present state of our relationships are, and, most important, what is going on in our own heads and hearts. Before leaping into action, it rarely hurts to ask oneself, What am I thinking, feeling, and wanting? If the task is to be accomplished effectively and safely, it will be especially important to answer these questions: On whom am I dependent? Who is dependent on me? With whom do I need to improve a relationship in order to improve communication?

PRACTICE BECOMING MORE MINDFUL

Reflection implies becoming more mindful. One of the original teachers of mindfulness is Ellen Langer, who coaches leaders to consider the context outside of a precipitating event or proximate cause.[9] Taking the time to wonder *What else is happening here?* or *What is different today?* takes our minds off obsessing on a problem or challenge and helps us to broaden our perspective on that challenge. It is not about denying the immediate feelings; it is about containing and compartmentalizing in order to see the broader context, which may look more like a net positive than a problem, or more like an opportunity than a challenge.

Humble Inquiry presumes continuous assessment of the situation, so asking oneself what else is happening may be an essential pre-condition for effective inquiry. We do not want to fall into the trap of not reflecting and then plowing in with a sequence of telling or leading questions that betray a lack of situational awareness. The tough boss who has always relied on telling may find, upon reflection, that he or she has the capacity and even the desire to try a different approach, such as going to a direct report and asking kindly, "What's on your mind today? Tell me about it . . ." Rather than adding more work to do that day, such inquiry might actually take some pressure off the workday at hand.

ENGAGE THE IMPROVISATIONAL ARTIST WITHIN YOU

Culture provides, if not imposes, scripts for our behavior, as we have discussed throughout this book. An artist's script involves painstaking observation to catch subtleties that might escape the casual onlooker but are often at the core of genuine experience. On the other hand, business scripts have traditionally glorified gut feelings and quick moves. We are encouraged to see contemporary leadership theory beginning to emphasize the kind of observation that has always been an integral tool for actors, painters, and other visual artists, leaving behind the myth that business success hinges on instincts and fast thinking.

Can Humble Inquiry—helping us hone a discipline of seeing and reflecting on the responses of others—help us to access the artist inside? All too often it feels awkward for participants to be thrown into artistic exercises, role-plays, and improvs. It is rare, however, for someone not to feel opened up and expanded by these kinds of exercises. It is not about whether the art is any good; it is about trying something new that challenges our scripts and broadens our perspective.

Conversations can be treated as art, and as such, can be subject to innovation. The Second City, the improv and comedy powerhouse that has introduced the world to countless superstars of comedy and acting, has a very simple axiom that fits perfectly with Humble Inquiry: "Yes, and"[10] (instead of "yes, but"). In a Second City context, "Yes, and" sets up the other person to deliver the punch line, to complete the story, to get the laughs. Starting with "Yes, and" in conversation builds on and reinforces, rather than negating or redirecting. "Yes, and" is your voice amplifying what the other person has said. The Second City folks refer to this as *explore and heighten*.[11] If your first impulse is to respond with "Yes, and," and you follow this with explore and heighten, your contribution to the conversation sets up the next contributor to further explore and heighten.

There is no substitute for doing something creative, even if it is only doodling, keeping a journal, or sitting around a campfire and engaging in inclusive and expansive dialogue. "Yes, and" with explore and heighten can create beautiful results, and even if the direct outcome is nothing notable, the learning process may have unique long-term benefits.

LEARN FROM YOUR OWN GROUP BEHAVIOR

If you learn to vary your pace and become more mindful, you will also want to find time for a particular form of reflection, which is to review and analyze something that you have just done. Effective groups review their decisions to see what can be learned. Many effective teams, even in complex hierarchies like the U.S. Armed Forces emphasize after-action reviews as a deliberate attempt to get feedback from everyone regardless of rank. Hospitals hold special post-op meetings to review cases, especially when things go wrong.

The *plus/delta* is a post-meeting variant of this process to highlight what went well (plus) and what did not go well and needs to change (delta). We have seen such process reviews provide invaluable learning and closure in improvement teams at health-care institutions. This may be in large part because the appointed leader can suspend any cultural norms of rank and deference and ask even the lowest-ranking teammates to speak openly about their perceptions of what has gone on. In those reviews, it is worth considering Humble Inquiry as the primary form of question to draw out insight from everyone. If the leader starts with Humble Inquiry and encourages all of the group members to stick with "Yes, and," the group can dramatically increase the chances of capturing all of the tidbits and insights for all to learn from. A shared insight is a terrible thing to waste.

In Conclusion

It can be hard for leaders, particularly new leaders, to accept their dependence on their teams of reports and peers and to embrace Here-and-now Humility, in order to build and reinforce relationships of high trust and openness. It may be countercultural, yet it may be the most important thing to learn.

How might these various suggestions help you, as a leader, to tackle this challenge? Reflecting more, becoming more mindful, perhaps even adding ten minutes of check-in before diving in to a formal meeting agenda, all can lead to better coordination and collaboration. Building open and trusting relationships is a more nebulous process, which can be very fast or may take some time. At its core, the process is personal and natural—you know how to do it! You start by deciding that maintaining professional distance is not particularly helpful if you are sure you need to collaborate to succeed.

It is always worth asking yourself "Can I afford to be so sure I know the answer that I do not need to adopt a Humble Inquiry attitude?" Situational awareness enables a leader or manager to be clearer about when he or she does have an answer and can afford to *tell*. Humble Inquiry empowers leaders and managers to be more sensitive in situations where more information is needed. The ultimate challenge is for you to discover that in those moments you *should not succumb to telling.* Now more than ever it's critical to keep inquiring to find the truth in context.

Notes

1. Johansen, B. (2020) *Full Spectrum Thinking: How to Escape Boxes in a Post-categorical Future.* Oakland, CA: Berrett-Koehler.

2. Edmondson, A. C. (2012) *Teaming: How Organizations Learn, Innovate, and Compete in the Knowledge Economy.* San Francisco, CA: Jossey-Bass/Wiley. Schein, E. H (2009). *Helping: How to Offer, Give and Receive Help.* Oakland, CA: Berrett-Koehler.

3. Potter, S. (1951) *Gamesmanship.* New York: Holt. Potter, S. (1952) *One-Upmanship.* New York: Holt.

4. Bailyn, L. (2006) *Breaking the Mold: Redesigning Work for Productive and Satisfying Lives.* Ithaca, NY: Cornell University Press.

5. Edmondson, A. (2012) *Teaming: How Organizations Learn, Innovate, and Compete in the Knowledge Economy.* San Francisco: Jossey-Bass/Wiley.

6. We introduced this word *personizing* in our book *Humble Leadership* (2019) to draw attention to the particular aspects of communication we use when we are building a Level 2 relationship, and we note that Humble Inquiry is perhaps the best example of such personizing.

7. Luft, J. (1961) "The Johari Window." *Human Relations Training News* 5 (1), pp. 6–7.

8. A good summary of the vast number of studies done on cognitive bias is McRaney, D. (2011) *You Are Not So Smart: Why You Have Too Many Friends on Facebook, Why Your Memory Is Mostly Fiction, and 46 Other Ways You're Deluding Yourself.* New York: Gotham Books. See also Ariely, D. (2008) *Predictably*

Irrational: The Hidden Forces That Shape Our Decisions. New York: Harper.

9. Langer, E. (1997) *The Power of Mindful Learning.* Reading, MA: Addison-Wesley.

10. Leonard, K., and Yorton, T. (2015) *Yes, And: How Improvisation Reverses "No, But" Thinking and Improves Creativity and Collaboration.* New York: HarperCollins.

11. Leonard and Yorton, ibid. p. 40

Discussion Guide and Exercises

General Discussion Questions

CHAPTER 1

The story about the graduate student being interrupted by his young daughter resonates for the simple reason that we've all been there in one form or another. In small discussion groups, try recounting a similar situation that you faced. What is common to these situations is that we either overreact or react incorrectly. What causes this? Is it our upbringing, the macroculture we have grown up in, stress and impatience? How can we understand irrational knee-jerk responses when the logic of Humble Inquiry is pretty clear?

CHAPTER 2

Consider the question "What's going on?" contrasted with the question "Everything going okay?" One of these questions is open and one is closed. Why does it matter? Because the second question can be answered with a simple *yes* or *no*, so it may not be helpful in building trust and openness. What are other examples of open questions that seem like good invitations to relationship building, or what are closed questions that may miss the mark, fall flat, or end up with conversation-stopping one-word answers?

CHAPTER 3

The implicit challenge of this chapter is this: while we present Humble Inquiry as the idealized optimal form of inquiry, there are many situations where process-oriented inquiry, as well as diagnostic and even confrontive inquiry, may be appropriate in specific contexts. Discuss situations in which process-oriented inquiry, diagnostic inquiry, or even confrontive questions may be the right first intervention. Can you defend this choice of question type?

CHAPTER 4

The culture of do and tell is how we see it. Do you agree? Some may view it as the culture of get-it-done-and-demonstrate-success or the culture of fail-fast-and-continuously-improve. Or is it the culture of command-and-control? Do those with power protect their power and not look back? These are all reasonable descriptions. How would you describe the cultural context within which you are hoping to succeed? How important is it that the attitude of Humble Inquiry is present in this context? If not, what kind of attitude in contrast to the Humble Inquiry attitude might be more successful?

CHAPTER 5

Like our distinction between telling and asking, we discuss the distinction between transactional relationships and personal relationships. Implicit in our argument is the proposition that personal (*personized*) relationships offer more flexibility and resiliency across a wide spectrum of tasks and challenges. Can you think of an instance where this is not—or was not—the case? Are there examples where a transactional relationship is better suited to the work now and in the future? Try developing a table of tasks and occupations that are better served by Level 1 transactional relationships (left column) versus Level 2 *personized* relationships (right column).

CHAPTER 6

Pair up with a friend or colleague you already trust. Review the Johari window together. First, what do each of you tend to conceal from each other about each other? Second, what do you see in each other that you assume the other does not see? (Do not try this unless you agree that you each want to learn more about the relationship and are willing to take some risks interpersonally and culturally.)

CHAPTER 7

Since each of us make all of the mistakes in the ORJI cycle at some time or other, the trick is to figure out in which part of the cycle we are most likely to "jump the gun" and make a mistake that then escalates in the rest of the cycle. Identify a set of situations that did not work out well and reconstruct backward which part of the cycle created the problem. Then working further backward, figure out whether the actual error had occurred in an even earlier part of the cycle. This reconstructive analysis often reveals that the real problem is in our perceptual biases, in step one.

CHAPTER 8

Focus on the critical distinction between *survival anxiety* as a motivator to change and *learning anxiety* as the resistance to change. Ask yourself why you do not use Humble Inquiry more. What about it scares you or does not come naturally? Is it that you have not found yourself in a situation that required such reflection, or is it that you did not want to take the time to humbly inquire? Can you think about situations in your immediate future that may not go well, where you may fail, if you do not adapt a Humble Inquiry attitude?

Twelve Mini Case Studies to Illustrate Humble Inquiry

Humble Inquiry is an attitude that can and should show up in different kinds of situations. The most important aspect of the attitude is *situational awareness*, assessing in every conversation what your purpose is and how it aligns to the situation at hand. You may just be exploring, having fun, or trying to convince someone of something; you may be trying to build a relationship or decipher what may really be going on if the situation is ambiguous or full of conflict. Everything you do next will be an intervention, even if you just stay in a silent observer mode, and will convey some aspect of your purpose to the other person in the conversation. It will help to learn to become mindful of the different consequences of what you say.

For each of the twelve situations that we describe below, ask yourself what you would say and make a note of it in the space provided. After you are done, read the several possible responses and how each relates to the concept of Humble Inquiry. You can then compare what you think you might have said to the various alternatives.

This is not a test and you don't get a score. This is an opportunity to observe yourself in action and become more mindful of how you operate.

1. A wife and husband in their 60s are concluding dinner. She/he says: "We could go out to a movie tonight...or go to the pub."

    How might you respond? _____

    _____

    _____

2. A family with school-age kids is finishing the dishes and getting ready for homework and reading. A ten-year-old boy says: "Mom (or Dad), can you help me with my math problem?"

    What do you say? _____

    _____

    _____

3. Two thirty-something friends are meeting for a glass of wine while their partners are at a meeting. One of them opens up with: "I am continuing to have an issue with my partner. He/she never seems to listen to me or to hear what I'm saying..."

    What do you say? _____

    _____

    _____

4. A patient arrives at a scheduled visit to discuss a nagging health issue—nothing serious, but it requires an office visit. The doctor arrives after a short wait. You are the doctor and kick off the visit.

    What do you say to open the appointment? _____

    _____

    _____

5. You are a manager running a team meeting and need progress reports on the team's projects because you are vaguely aware that the team is falling behind, but you are not at all sure why. You are opening the task portion of the meeting.

   What do you say? _____

   _____

   _____

6. You have a new job assignment for one of your direct reports, but you are not sure the direct report will enthusiastically accept this new assignment. You can position it as a promotion, though you are still not sure it will be accepted.

   How do you present this opportunity ? _____

   _____

   _____

7. Your spouse tells you: "I had a big fight with our neighbor this afternoon."

   What do you say? _____

   _____

   _____

8. Your fellow team members are becoming noticeably less engaged in weekly staff meetings, and you are not sure why. As a team member you are worried about this. You are at a meeting where the boss is not present.

   What do you say or do? _____

   _____

   _____

9. Your boss calls you into the office to tell you the new plan for the team project. You see some real flaws in the plan.

   What do you say? _____

   _____

   _____

10. In a staff meeting, one of your peers is misrepresenting your work in order to cast a more favorable light on his or her work. You feel you need to confront this issue.

   What do you say? _____

   _____

   _____

11. You are aware of some delays in new product development in one of your product teams. You need to know what is going on, but you are not sure the team will be forthcoming in telling you honestly about the hard truth of the situation.

   What do you say? _____

   _____

   _____

12. You are the newly promoted manager of a project team. You know the other team members based on their résumés, but this is your first actual face-to-face meeting with them. They are gathered in the conference room waiting for you. You enter.

   What do you say? _____

   _____

   _____

Possible Responses

Our hypothetical answers are not presented to imply that any one of them is correct and the others are wrong. Our intent is to illustrate the differences between Humble Inquiry and the other alternatives we have discussed in this book. You can try covering the right column to see if you agree with our assessments of the kinds of responses.

Again, the purpose of this exercise is not to give yourself a score but to encourage you to think about your reactions in these various conversational situations.

1.   A wife and husband in their 60s are concluding dinner. She/he says: "We could go out to a movie tonight...or go to the pub." How might you respond?

Some options

"Sounds like you want to get out of the house. Sorry, I have some work to do. Perhaps another night..."	A tell response
"Sure, I would like to do something, but why do you want to see a movie?"	Diagnostic Inquiry (assimilating data)
"Sure, let's figure something out. What's on your mind—a movie, an outing, or *something else*?"	Humble Inquiry (getting to the truth of what is going on)

2.   A family with school-age kids is finishing the dishes and getting ready for homework and reading. A ten-year-old boy says: "Mom (or Dad), can you help me with my math problem?" What do you say?

Some options

"Show me the problem. Okay, I'll show you how to do that..."	A tell response

"Let's take a few minutes and talk after dinner..."	Humble Inquiry (trying to get at the truth of what is going on—is it really just about the math problem?)
"Again tonight? Seems like long division is really stumping you. I remember it being tricky but fun when you get the hang of it."	Confrontive inquiry and content seduction (assuming it is really about the math)

3. Two thirty-something friends are meeting for a glass of wine while their partners are at a meeting. One of them opens up with: "I am continuing to have an issue with my partner. He/she never seems to listen to me or to hear what I'm saying..." What do you say?

Some options

"Ouch, I'm sorry to hear that. Can you tell me more?"	Humble Inquiry and empathy (getting at the truth of what is going on)
"Are you sure you want to talk about this right now?"	Process-oriented inquiry (are they both ready to dig into this?)
"Have you confronted her/him with your feeling?"	Confrontive inquiry (implied tell and unsolicited implied advice)
"I would call him/her out. Let him/her know how you feel. Be direct."	A straight tell response

4. A patient arrives at a scheduled visit to discuss a nagging health issue—nothing serious, but it requires an office visit. The doctor arrives after a short wait. You are the doctor and kick off the visit. What do you say to open the appointment?

Some options

"Any new symptoms or patterns you can tell me about?"	Diagnostic inquiry
"Have you been following the food and exercise regimen we discussed last time?"	A tell response
"How are things going? What's on your mind?"	Humble Inquiry (getting at the truth of what is going on)

5. You are a manager running a team meeting and need progress reports on the team's projects because you are vaguely aware that the team is falling behind, but you are not at all sure why. You are opening the task portion of the meeting. What do you say?

Some options

"We need to resolve all the yellows and reds on these dashboards. We look bad if we can't resolve them quickly. Tim, looks like you have some work to do…"	A tell response
"Let's get right to the progress reports, one by one. Tim, your dashboard is showing 'red' on salesforce readiness. Can you fill us in on your plan to get that metric to 'green'?"	Diagnostic inquiry (assimilating data) focusing on one member
"We have lots of specifics to cover, and I'd like to start by each of you taking a few moments to share what's going on with your key projects."	Humble Inquiry (creating an interpersonal context that permits finding out together what is causing the issues)

6. You have a new job assignment for one of your direct reports, but you are not sure the direct report will enthusiastically accept this new assignment. You can position it as a promotion, though you are still not sure it will be accepted. How do you present this opportunity?

   Some options

"I am going to reassign you to the XYZ division. This will be a highly visible move for you, basically a promotion. I hope you are as thrilled as I am!"	A tell response
"I have a new assignment to propose to you. I think it is a great move and effectively a promotion. Would you have any objection to taking over coverage for the XYZ division?"	Diagnostic inquiry (in search of objections)
"How are you doing with your current assignments—are things working out? Would you be interested in some different opportunities? Are there any divisional assignments that interest you?"	Humble Inquiry (finding the right fit, getting at what really motivates this direct report)

7. Your spouse tells you: "I had a big fight with our neighbor this afternoon." What do you say?

   Some options

"Are they complaining again about our new fence?"	A tell response (in the form of a question)
"Did you win?"	Confrontive inquiry
"Tell me more…"	Humble Inquiry (making it safe for your spouse to let it all out)

8. Your fellow team members are becoming noticeably less engaged in weekly staff meetings, and you are not sure why. As a team member you are worried about this. You are at a meeting where the boss is not present. What do you say or do?

Some options

"I think we are not working hard enough. Let's get with it!"	A clear tell
"How is everyone feeling about these meetings?"	Humble Inquiry (making it safe to air it out) but be mindful that it could spiral down into all feelings and no commitment to improve—a vent session with no productive outcome
"Do some of you share my feelings that we need to work harder?"	Diagnostic inquiry

9. Your boss calls you into the office to tell you the new plan for the team project. You see some real flaws in the plan. What do you say?

Some options

"I am concerned there might be some problems with this. Can we talk it through?"	Humble Inquiry (taking the chance at revealing your doubts)
"Well, sounds okay to me…"	A tell (you would tell if you could, but it's not psychologically safe)
"I'm not sure. What are the others saying?"	Diagnostic inquiry (on safe ground)

10. In a staff meeting, one of your peers is misrepresenting your work in order to cast a more favorable light on his or her work. You feel you need to confront this issue. What do you say?

Some options

(In a one-on-one with the peer) "What's going on? Can you see how this information might be harmful to me? When you present it that way, I feel threatened. How can we resolve this?"	Process-oriented inquiry (validating feelings, revealing own feelings)
(In a team meeting directed at the peer) "I do not think that data is accurate. Where did you get that information, because it conflicts with what I am seeing? Have you verified it?"	Confrontive inquiry (girding for a fight)
(In a team meeting) "Can we reconstruct together how we got to this point?"	Humble Inquiry and process-oriented inquiry (creating an interpersonal context that permits finding out together what is causing the issues)
(In a team meeting directed at the peer) "Your data is wrong. There is no way your results are that much better than my results. Let's get real here—your results are not real."	A tell response

11. You are aware of some delays in new product development in one of your product teams. You need to know what is going on, but you are not sure the team will be forthcoming in telling you honestly about the hard truth of the situation. What do you say?

Some options

"I'm picking up some vibes that one of our new product initiatives is hitting delays. I need to know what is going on so that I can position it properly for our division VP. Can you tell me exactly what is going on?"	Confrontive inquiry (you need to know)
"I am more concerned about how we are working together as a team than any specific bit of good or bad news. I will represent us to the division VP when we are all clear on what's going on with the new product initiatives."	Humble Inquiry (getting to the truth of what is going on and advancing some degree of accountability sharing)
"All of our jobs are on the line if these new product initiatives are delayed. We must get them back on track."	A tell response

12. You are the newly promoted manager of a project team. You know the other team members based on their résumés, but this is your first actual face-to-face meeting with them. They are gathered in the conference room waiting for you. You enter. What do you say?

Some options

"Hi, my name is Joe/Joan Smith, and I have been asked to take over this project. I looked over all your résumés and know we have a great team here. This is an important project that I am sure you will find challenging, so I am looking forward to working with all of you on this. Let's do a brief round of intros and get to work."	A straight tell (no sense of genuine interest in finding out who is on the team)

"Hi, I'm glad to finally meet all of you. I like to be called Joe/Joan and am very excited to be working with you on this important project and here is why: (explains reasons). Let's all get on the same page by going around the room once and each of us tell what it is about this project that appeals to you. Add anything about yourself if you feel like it, so we can start off by getting to know each other."

A complicated Humble Inquiry response (revealing self and inviting others to be open about themselves, in effect, testing the degree to which the group members feel safe to be open)

"Hi, I'm glad to finally meet all of you. Now that we are together as a team, I would like to hear from you what you have done so far. Could you brief me..."

Diagnostic inquiry (assumes that the team members feel psychologically safe to open up)

"Hi, I'm glad to finally meet all of you. I'm the new kid on the block here, so to get us started, would you bring me up to speed by telling me a bit about the history of this group, what's been going on, and how I can help move things forward..."

Pure Humble Inquiry (the person in charge is clearly making himself/herself vulnerable)

Acknowledgments

As co-authors of this revision we want to again acknowledge the people who helped to create the first edition. The most helpful were Daniel Asnes, Karen Ayas, Lotte Bailyn, David Coughlan, Tina Doerffer, Jody Gittell, Tom Huber, Mary Jane Kornacki, Bob McKersie, Philip Mix, Joichi Ogawa, Jack Silversin, Emily Sper, John Van Maanen, and Ilene Wasserman. We also acknowledge Bob Johansen for his insights about the future, and of course the Berrett-Koehler reviewers who provided detailed comments and suggestions.

Concepts and ideas grow out of experience, so we are indebted to our clients whose stories illustrate so well the importance of Humble Inquiry in today's world. In particular we cannot overstate our gratitude to leaders and innovators in the infinitely complex world of health care in the United States, especially at Stanford Health Care. In our work with organizations, we have rarely seen greater challenges faced than in health care during a pandemic. Health care providers spend every working hour at the confluence of experimentation and procedure, of decisiveness and compassion, of known unknowns and unknown unknowns. And they do this humbly caring for patients who may be facing their last challenge. They provide medical help to humanity, but perhaps even more important, they endeavor to provide health care *with humanity*.

Finally, we both give thanks to the many friends, clients, and strangers who helped us to see the less constructive side of *telling*, and even more importantly, the beauty of how to humbly inquire to help people and lead them forward.

Ed and Peter Schein
Palo Alto, CA, September 2020

Index

Page numbers with *f* refer to figures, *t* to tables, and *n* to notes.

About the Authors

ED SCHEIN is Professor Emeritus of the Massachusetts Institute of Technology (MIT) Sloan School of Management. He was educated at the University of Chicago, Stanford University, and Harvard University, where he received his PhD in Social Psychology in 1952. He worked at the Walter Reed Institute of Research for four years and then joined MIT, where he taught until 2005. He has published extensively—*Organizational Psychology*, 3rd ed. (1980); *Process Consultation Revisited* (1999); *Career Dynamics* (1978); *Career Anchors*, 4th ed., with John Van Maanen (2013). He also wrote a cultural analysis of Singapore's economic miracle (*Strategic*

Pragmatism, 1996) and a book about the rise and fall of Digital Equipment Corp. (*DEC Is Dead; Long Live DEC*, 2003). Ed and his son Peter Schein have co-authored many papers and books including *Organizational Culture and Leadership*, 5th ed. (2017), *Humble Leadership* (2018, A Nautilus Book Awards Silver Medal winner), and *The Corporate Culture Survival Guide*, 3rd ed. (2019).

In 2009 Ed published *Helping*, a book on the general theory and practice of giving and receiving help, followed in 2013 by the first edition of *Humble Inquiry*, which won a 2014 leadership book award from the Department of Leadership of the University of San Diego. He published *Humble Consulting* in 2016, which revises the whole model of how to consult and coach, and is working with his son Peter on various projects in their Organizational Culture and Leadership Institute (OCLI.org).

Ed is the 2009 recipient of the Distinguished Scholar-Practitioner Award from the Academy of Management, the 2012 recipient of the Lifetime Achievement Award from the International Leadership Association, and the 2015 Lifetime Achievement Award in Organization Development from the International OD Network. In addition, he has an Honorary Doctorate from the IEDC Bled School of Management in Slovenia.

PETER SCHEIN is the co-founder and COO of OCLI.org in Menlo Park, California. He provides counsel to senior management on organizational development challenges facing private and public sector entities worldwide. He is a contributing author to the 5th edition of *Organizational Culture and Leadership* (Schein, 2017) and co-author of *Humble Leadership* (2018) and *The Corporate Culture Survival Guide*, 3rd ed. (2019).

Peter's work draws on 30 years of industry experience in marketing and corporate development at technology pioneers. In his early career he developed new products at Pacific Bell and Apple. He led product efforts at Silicon Graphics, Inc., Concentric Network Corporation (XO Communications), and Packeteer (Blue Coat). Thereafter, Peter spent 11 years in corporate development and strategy at Sun Microsystems, where he led investments in high-growth ecosystems. He drove acquisitions of technology innovators that developed into highly valued product lines at Sun. Through these experiences developing new strategies organically, and merging smaller entities into a large company, Peter developed a keen focus on the underlying organizational development challenges that growth engenders in innovation-driven enterprises.

Peter was educated at Stanford University (BA Social Anthropology, with Honors and Distinction), Northwestern University (Kellogg MBA, Marketing and Information Management), and the USC Marshall School of Business (HCEO Certificate).

Also by Edgar H. Schein and Peter A. Schein

Humble Leadership
The Power of Relationships, Openness, and Trust

Leadership is a relationship—but that relationship must change, say legendary organizational scholar Edgar Schein and former Silicon Valley executive Peter Schein. The vertical hierarchy, with its emphasis on formal, transactional relationships, professional distance, and all guidance coming from the top, is hopelessly inflexible and outdated. In a complex world, leadership must rely on high levels of trust and openness throughout the organization, and these can be achieved only by what the authors call personization and Level 2 relationships, which build the agility to make course corrections quickly. This book shows how such humble leadership has built effective cultures in a whole range of sectors: health care, government, the military, tech and innovation, and more.

Paperback, ISBN 978-1-5230-9538-4
PDF ebook, ISBN 978-1-5230-9539-1
ePub ebook, ISBN 978-1-5230-9540-7
Digital audio, ISBN 978-1-5230-9542-1

Berrett–Koehler Publishers, Inc.
www.bkconnection.com   **800.929.2929**

Also by Edgar H. Schein and Peter A. Schein

Humble Consulting
How to Provide Real Help Faster

Edgar Schein argues that consultants have to work with their clients in a more personal way, emphasizing authentic openness, curiosity, and humility. Schein draws deeply on his own decades of experience, offering over two dozen case studies that illuminate each stage of this humble consulting process.

Paperback, ISBN 978-1-62656-720-7
PDF ebook, ISBN 978-1-62656-721-4
ePub ebook, ISBN 978-1-62656-722-1
Digital audio, ISBN 978-1-62656-724-5

Helping
How to Offer, Give, and Receive Help

Helping others is one of the most universal things that people do every day in their work and lives. Yet often this help is not helpful or is resented or refused. In this seminal book, a preeminent author and scholar analyzes the dynamics of helping relationships and shows how to provide help that is really helpful.

Hardcover, ISBN 978-1-57675-863-2
Paperback, ISBN 978-1-60509-856-2
PDF ebook, ISBN 978-1-57675-872-4
ePub ebook, ISBN 978-1-60509-880-7
Digital audio, ISBN 978-1-5230-8813-3

Berrett–Koehler Publishers, Inc.
www.bkconnection.com   **800.929.2929**

Dear reader,

Thank you for picking up this book and welcome to the worldwide BK community! You're joining a special group of people who have come together to create positive change in their lives, organizations, and communities.

What's BK all about?

Our mission is to connect people and ideas to create a world that works for all.

Why? Our communities, organizations, and lives get bogged down by old paradigms of self-interest, exclusion, hierarchy, and privilege. But we believe that can change. That's why we seek the leading experts on these challenges—and share their actionable ideas with you.

A welcome gift

To help you get started, we'd like to offer you a **free copy** of one of our bestselling ebooks:

www.bkconnection.com/welcome

When you claim your **free ebook**, you'll also be subscribed to our blog.

Our freshest insights

Access the best new tools and ideas for leaders at all levels on our blog at ideas.bkconnection.com.

Sincerely,

Your friends at Berrett-Koehler

Certified

Corporation